THE GHOSTS

THE GHOSTS

ANTONIA BARBER

Farrar, Straus & Giroux
New York

An Ariel Book

For Ken

Part One

∞∞∞∞∞∞∞∞∞∞∞∞∞∞∞∞∞∞∞∞∞∞∞∞∞∞∞∞∞∞∞∞∞

1

IF IT had not been such a rain-lashed, windy evening, the people who jostled the pavements of Camden Town might have noticed something a little odd about a white-haired elderly gentleman who made his way against the steady flow of the crowd. But they shivered as they left the warm brightness of the Underground station and, burying their chins deep in the lapels of their coats, butted their way out into the driving rain seeing nothing but the puddled pavements and a great multitude of hurrying feet.

Perhaps the strangest thing about the old man was that he walked upright, untroubled by the cold needles of the rain. And though he moved against the press of the crowd, he never once stepped aside, but passed through the groups of burly workmen, the thin-faced office boys, the breathless, scampering girls, without seeming to touch any of them.

He moved purposefully, past the neon-lit self-service laundry and the shuttered fish-shop, past the busy greengrocer's spilling its wooden boxes and pyramids of bright fruit across the pavement outside, until he reached a row of terraced houses which stood back from the road behind wilderness gardens. Here he paused uncertainly and stared at the first house which lay in a pool of shadow behind a stunted tree. A small light shone from the basement window, making a halo of brightness on the rain outside. The old man turned and, making his way along the path and down the steps, he tapped hesitantly upon the basement door.

The woman who opened it was still young and would have been pretty if she had not looked so tired.

"Mrs ... er ... Mrs Allen?" inquired the old man. He sounded strangely nervous.

The woman nodded cautiously and at once he launched into a little speech like a doorstep salesman uncertain of his reception. "I represent a firm of solicitors, madam, the firm of Blunden, Blunden, Claverton and ... "

"I suppose it's about the rent."

The woman's interruption seemed to throw the old man completely. He stopped his speech abruptly and looked deeply hurt at being suspected of so unwelcome a mission. He shook his head several times reproachfully and seemed to have difficulty in finding the broken thread of his thoughts.

"Indeed no!" he said at last. "I am not a debt-collector. I am a senior partner in the firm of Blunden, Blunden, Claverton and ... dear me ... now what is that young fellow's name ... ?" He paused absent-mindedly and gazed up thoughtfully into the falling rain. "Well, no matter," — he recollected himself — "the important thing is that the news I bring will, I am sure, prove entirely welcome."

The woman looked doubtful, as if she no longer believed in good news. Then she shivered: it was cold standing in the doorway. "You'd better come in," she said, "out of the rain."

The room was small and crowded and untidy. There was a pool of light over a table to one side where a boy and a girl sat eating their tea. The boy started to his feet as they came in but the old man stopped him. "No, no!" he said with grave courtesy, "pray continue. It is I who must apologize for disturbing your meal."

"Do sit down," said the woman, moving some knitting from a chair by the fire, "and perhaps you would like a cup of tea?"

"The chair I accept gratefully," said the old man, "but the tea I must decline. It is many years since I have been ... er ... allowed to drink it. But if you will pour some for yourself and sit with me for a moment, I will come straight to the purpose of my visit."

The woman did as she was told. Clutching her cup in nervous hands, she perched herself on the edge of a chair and waited as if for another blow to fall.

The children ate steadily, watching their mother and their unexpected visitor with unmoving eyes. The boy thought: He's a weird old thing. His clothes are so old-fashioned and he talks like someone out of *David Copperfield*. The girl noticed that his clothes were not steaming in the heat of the fire. They seemed to be quite dry although he had not carried an umbrella. But it was only a small fire, she told herself, and as he was outside the circle of the overhead light, it was hard to be certain whether he was wet or not.

"I will not ... er ... stand upon ceremony," the old man began. "I shall come ... er ... straight to the point ... " But he seemed curiously reluctant to do so.

The boy wondered if he was an encyclopedia salesman. If

9

he is, he thought, he's wasting his time on us. We couldn't afford a Penguin between us.

But when the old man finally overcame his embarrassment enough to finish his sentence, it turned out that he was offering not twenty-eight matched volumes, but a job or rather, as he put it, 'a responsible position'.

Mrs Allen was so surprised that she could not answer at first, and misunderstanding her silence the old man said anxiously, "I trust I have not offended you by making such a suggestion. I realize that a lady like yourself ... " He paused miserably and then added by way of apology, "I had reason to believe that the ... er ... money might be useful to you."

The woman took pity on him: she gave him a sad smile, half of gratitude and half of disappointment. "Why should I be offended?" she asked. "It is true that the money would be very useful and I have often thought of taking a job, but I have the baby to consider. He's not a year old yet and he has never been very strong. I couldn't leave him with strangers while I went out to work."

"No, no, of course not!" said the old man soothingly. "That is why the position I mention would be most suitable for you. Perhaps you would allow me to explain a little further?"

Mrs Allen nodded and he went on, "My firm is seeking a reliable person to act as ... er ... as caretaker to a property which is in our charge. The last owner, a Mr Latimer, died some time ago without direct heirs and we are endeavouring to trace more distant relatives. So far, alas, we have met with little success and indeed it seems at times that there are none surviving. In the meantime, the house must be cared for, and for ...er ... various reasons we have had difficulty in finding anyone willing to take the post. It is the ... um ... the remoteness, you understand. It is a very fine house and pleasantly situated but it stands alone some way from the nearest village. There is a rent-free, caretaker's cottage attached to the house and your duties would be very light, nothing more than a regular inspection of the house to see that all is in order. A woman comes up from the village to do what cleaning is necessary and the local builder is at hand for any repairs that may be required, but we are anxious that there should be someone living on the premises at all times."

The old man paused. The woman said nothing. She seemed almost unable to grasp what he was saying, unable to believe in an offer that so completely answered all her needs.

"The country air would be most beneficial to the children," he continued, "and the remoteness may, perhaps, encourage you to concentrate on your music." He hesitated a moment and then added enticingly, "There is a very fine piano in the music-room."

The girl stopped eating and stared at the old man. How had he known that their mother had once ... ?

Mrs Allen said abruptly, "I don't play any more. I haven't played for a long time, not since ... " Her voice trailed away.

"Not since your husband's death," prompted the old man gently and she nodded without speaking. "It was a tragic accident ... A tragic accident," he repeated, "and our loss as well as your own. It is rare to find a young man with such great talent."

The widow's pride overcame her sadness. "They had only

just begun to realize how good he was," she said. "We were so thrilled when he was invited to conduct some of his own music in New York."

"Ah, yes, indeed," said the old man. "It must have given him a particular satisfaction to know that his work was appreciated in his own country."

"Yes, it did, especially since he had been away for so long. We met in Paris, you know, when we were both students" — she smiled as she remembered — "and after we were married and the children were born, we decided to settle in London. Dick had no close relatives in the States and he was happy here. He used to say that he was a throw-back because he felt so much at home in England."

Listening to the conversation, the boy had grown uneasy. He wondered how the old man came to know so much about them. He had obviously been snooping around asking questions, but why? and why had he chosen them? Perhaps he was looking for a family with no relatives to miss them. He would lure them all to this dark old house, and they would never be heard of again. He remembered a book he had once read about a mad old professor …

The girl was watching her mother and she marvelled to see her talking so freely of the husband who was dead. She never talks to anyone about him, she thought, not even to us. The past is like a room with a locked door that we must never open. And yet she was talking away to the old man, almost as if she were talking to herself, almost as if he was not really there.

"He wanted to take us all with him, but of course we couldn't afford it and I was expecting the baby, so he went alone." She was silent for a moment, then she began again in a rush of words. "When the cable came we were all so excited. We thought it must be good news, you see, and then, when we saw ... a car-crash ... " She seemed to be on the point of tears and the girl rose quietly and went to put her arm round her mother's shoulders. The movement startled her, as if she had forgotten the children; she even glanced at the old man with some surprise as though she had indeed been talking to herself. "Well," she said awkwardly, "I haven't felt like playing since then."

The old man sighed. "You have my deepest sympathy," he said, "but you must try to believe me when I say that time will heal your grief."

The woman made no answer but almost unconsciously shook her head.

"You don't believe me now, but you will find that it is true. I am an old man ... a very old man ... and I have learned wisdom the hard way. It is not grief that scars, but guilt; not the blows we suffer, but the injuries we do to others ... " His words faded and there was a long silence. Then he seemed to recollect his mission. He leaned forward into the light of the fire. "Come now," he said earnestly, "grasp this opportunity if only for the children's sakes, to take them away from this place."

The woman reddened slightly, feeling the criticism that his words implied. She glanced around the room with its gloomy paintwork and damp-stained walls. "It is awful, isn't it," she said, "but it was the best I could find. Housing is such a problem when you have children. There were so many debts and so little money. Dick wasn't one to plan ahead. He used to joke and say that musicians and artists are the lilies of the field and that God provides for them."

"Perhaps He does," said the old man, "perhaps He does..."

Suddenly the woman smiled and the boy, watching her from the table corner, saw again for a moment why he had always thought her beautiful. She glanced up at the old man and asked, "Did He send you directly?"

But he seemed strangely flustered by the suggestion. "No, no!" he said, "I am only an old man anxious to help." He seemed to withdraw into himself. "But He moves in so mysterious a way," he muttered, "it is possible that even I, unworthy as I am, may serve some purpose." A look of deep gloom spread over his face.

"I'm sorry," said the woman gently. "I didn't mean to distress you. But if you mean your offer of a house and a job, then to us you are a Godsend."

Before the old man could answer, the sound of a baby's piercing cry came from the back room.

Mrs Allen rose to her feet anxiously. "Oh, dear," she said, "he's had such a cold and I think he suffers from earache. Please excuse me while I do something for him," and she hurried from the room.

Left behind, the children and their visitor sat in an uncomfortable silence.

After a while, the old man cleared his throat as if he were about to speak. Then he glanced anxiously at the children and cleared his throat again. But he said nothing.

The girl, feeling it her duty to put him at his ease, gathered up her courage and asked, "Are you sure you wouldn't like a cup of tea?"

"Thank you ... um ... er ... Lucy, my dear. It doesn't agree with me, I fear. But I wonder," he paused and seemed to search for the right words, "now that we are alone I wonder if I might ask you both a question. I hesitate because it is rather an unusual question and I hope that you will consider it seriously."

"Of course," said the boy cheerfully, "you fire away," but he thought: if he asks whether we have any surviving relatives, I shall know just what he's up to.

But the question took even him by surprise. "Do you think you would be afraid," asked the old man cautiously, "if you saw ... um ... er, that is to say, if you saw ... a ghost?"

Lucy stopped trying to work out how he had known her name and shivered. But she considered the question seriously as he had asked. She decided that she would be absolutely terrified but she wasn't going to admit that in front of her brother so she said, "I think I should be just a little bit scared."

The boy thought her answer very dull. "I think it would really depend on what kind of ghost it was," he said. "I mean if it was just wandering around in a white sheet moaning a bit, well, it would be all right, wouldn't it? But I once read a story about a man who was going along a dark lane one night when he saw a figure in a long dark cloak and hood." He warmed to his subject, never noticing the growing gloom on the old man's face. "Well, just when he was passing it the ghost, because it was a ghost, of course, turned round and threw back the cloak and it had no head, just a sort of grinning emptiness and below it a grisly skeleton. He screamed and ran away but it came after him and he felt its bony hand on his shoulder and ... "

"I think that's a lot of nonsense!" interrupted Lucy. She could see that the old man didn't like the story and she wasn't keen herself. She knew that she would remember it if she woke up in the night. "After all," she said scornfully, "how could it grin if it had no head?"

The boy looked annoyed and the old man intervened.

"It was not that sort of ghost that I had in mind, James, and indeed I do not believe that there are such visions. These ghosts would appear to you ... well, very much like ordinary people: children of about your own age, perhaps, or even" – he laughed creakily – "an old man such as myself."

"Oh, we wouldn't be frightened of a ghost like that." Jamie was confident to the point of scorn. "I mean you wouldn't know they were ghosts, would you? unless, of course, you could see through them and even that wouldn't be very scary if their heads were in the right place."

Lucy said nothing. She was looking at the old man closely: his narrow trousers would not have looked out of place on a teenager but they seemed odd for a man of his age. And there was something about his collar and the high folded cravat ... He was gazing absently into the fire.

"Sometimes," he began, "ghosts are people who come back seeking help. They are people who, during their lives, were not strong enough ... or wise enough ... or good enough to meet some challenge. They come seeking help because they cannot rest for the knowledge that they did harm and the longing to put it right ... " His words were so soft they might have passed for an uneasy sighing but Lucy heard them. She dimly understood that he was talking about himself, but because he sounded so very sad, she was not afraid.

16

"We would help you if we could," she said timidly.

The old man raised his head and she found herself gazing into dark, strangely transparent eyes. She shivered involuntarily and then smiled to make up for it.

The old man nodded. "I think you understand," he said. "Children do sometimes, but as they grow older they become less sensitive. They lose the power to believe ... to believe ... in the unlikely." He seemed to be murmuring to himself. "Once the meaning of words ... have set rigidly in the mind, the incredible becomes the unbelievable ... the possible and the impossible are irremediably sundered by a brief prefix..."

The children listened in silence, having only the vaguest idea of what he was talking about, but pleased to find that he seemed to approve of them.

The old man made a sudden effort and gathered his thoughts. "When you come to the house," he told them, "you will hear strange tales. They will tell you in the village that it is haunted, but you must not be afraid. When the time comes ... you will know what to do."

"We shan't be afraid," said Jamie firmly, and Lucy added, "We will do what we can."

"Thank you," said the old man solemnly and he rose to his feet. "I must not stay," he said. "I fear I have already been too long."

"Shall I fetch Mummy?" asked Lucy politely.

"No time," said the old man nervously, "no time! But if you will ask her to call at my chambers tomorrow ... " He moved in haste towards the door as though he might miss a train if he delayed.

"Where is it?" asked Jamie.

"Sensible child ... " The old man paused as Lucy opened the door. Fumbling in his pocket he produced a thin, yellowing card.

Jamie took it and read it and asked, "Will you be there?"

The old man shook his head. "I am ... er, that is I was ... " He seemed at a loss for words and Jamie suggested, "Retired?"

"Retired!" The old man gave a sad, hollow laugh. "Ah, if it were only so, an honourable retirement ... But alas, the truth must be told: I am, or rather I was ... struck off!" He spoke the words in a whisper as if it was the most terrible thing in the world, but Jamie was quite relieved.

"Is that all?" he said. "I thought for a moment that you were going to say that you were dead!"

"Dead!" exclaimed the old man mournfully. "Why, death is nothing. To be dead is a mere detail, but to be struck off is the most shameful thing of all." He stood in the doorway, shaking his head sadly, and all the time he seemed to grow more frail and insubstantial. "Tomorrow," he said and his voice was faint. "Tell them ... I sent you ... Claverton will be there ... or young ... what's ... his ... name ... "

Then he moved out into the shadowy garden and the wind and rain seemed to blow him away.

2

LUCY poked her finger into the baby's padded woollen tummy and watched him crow with delight. He thrust up his little thin arms at her and bubbled affection. She laughed and poked him again.

"You two sound very happy."

At the sound of her mother's voice Lucy withdrew her finger hastily. I don't know why I should feel guilty, she thought; but she did, perhaps because her mother could not hide the undertone of reproach in her voice. It isn't that she doesn't want us to be happy, thought Lucy; she just can't understand how we can be, now that he is dead. It's not so bad for us because we are old enough to understand, but it's not fair to the baby. She loves him but she can't play with him or laugh at him and, after all, it's not his fault. She turned to look at her mother and seeing her lined face, went to put her arms around her.

"He's only a baby," she said defensively, "and I do love to hear him laugh."

Her mother hugged her and looked down at her wriggling son. "My poor darlings," she said.

Lucy changed the subject. "What did Mrs Ryan say?"

"Oh, she'll be glad to keep an eye on him but I still wish I didn't have to leave him. She's always so busy with all those children and she is a bit slap-dash. But it's too cold to take him out, so there's nothing else for it. I only hope he doesn't get one of those coughing fits; they wouldn't even hear him with all that noise going on."

Lucy thought the baby would love the cheerful rough-and-tumble of the Ryan household but she could see that her mother would worry so she said, "Why don't you let me stay with him?"

"Well, I don't know ... " Mrs Allen hesitated. "A house in the country, it's such a chance for us, but I'm sure they'll turn me down when they find there are three children."

"The old man seemed certain that you would get it."

"I know, Lucy, but you tell me he won't even be there. Suppose they didn't know when they sent him that there were three children?"

"He seemed to know an awful lot about us," Lucy pointed out.

Mrs Allen frowned and considered. "No," she said, "I think you and Jamie had better come with me. People never believe you when you say that your children are quiet and well-behaved, but perhaps if they see you ... "

The door opened again and Jamie came in, loaded with shopping.

"Phew!" he said. "This lot weighs a ton but it's mostly potatoes. I got everything on the list and there's one-and-threepence change. I've almost given up Carter's Stores, you know; there's always a penny more on everything."

Shopping was Jamie's personal chore and he regarded it as a price war between himself and the local shopkeepers. He brought back the food like the spoils of battle and his change like a trophy.

"You'd better put a clean shirt on," said his mother as she stacked the groceries in the corner cupboard. "And we mustn't be long; I couldn't bear it if someone else got there first. You have got the card with the address on it, haven't you?"

Jamie fished in his pocket and brought out the small square of yellowed pasteboard. "Blunden, Blunden and Claverton, 7 Old Square Chambers, Lincoln's Inn," he read from the fine copper plate. He frowned, "Now I wonder what could have happened to young whatsit?"

The sign on the polished brass plate said: Blunden, Claverton and Smith.

"I suppose it is the same firm?" said Mrs Allen doubtfully, already suspecting that the whole thing had been a dream.

"Of course it is," said Lucy reassuringly. "Smith is the one the old man couldn't remember."

"Ah!" said Jamie solemnly, "and what became of the second Mr Blunden, that's what I want to know?"

"It might have been the first Mr Blunden," Lucy pointed out.

"Oh no, I'm sure our old man was the first Mr Blunden, and he seemed all right."

"Yes, but he did say he had been ... "

"James, Lucy, please! I've brought you along to show them how sensible you are. Don't start one of your foolish arguments."

The children's faces fell. They could tell from the sharp

edge on her voice how much the interview meant to their mother. Jamie took her hand and squeezed it.

"Sorry," he said. "We'll be absolute angels."

She gave him a nervous smile. "I know, Jamie, but we mustn't hope for too much."

They made their way up a dark staircase until they found the names again on a glass door. After a moment's hesitation, Mrs Allen drew a deep breath and they went in.

The room was larger and grander than they had expected from the outside, with sombre panelling on the walls. A young clerk rose from a desk at one side and came smoothly to meet them.

Mrs Allen went momentarily to pieces. "I've come about the job," she began, "a caretaker, Mr Blunden told us ... "

The young man raised one eyebrow in a rather superior way and said, "You have come about a job?"

Mrs Allen pulled herself together. "I understand," she said coolly, "that you are looking for a caretaker for a rather remote country house."

The young man looked surprised. "The job has not yet been advertised," he said disapprovingly, "how did you come to ... "

"Mr Blunden himself informed me of the vacancy and advised me to call on you. He gave me his card."

Her mother's manner was, thought Lucy, a shade uppity, but it seemed to impress the young man. Or perhaps it was the sight of old Mr Blunden's card; he was staring hard enough at it.

Jamie wondered whether the young man was Smith and if he was upset at finding his name omitted.

The young man looked up from the card. "I see," he said, in the puzzled tones of one who obviously did not see. "You must forgive me if I was a trifle abrupt. Mr Blunden has not been at the office recently and I did not realize that he had taken a hand in this matter. If you will let me have your name, I will inform Mr Claverton that you are here."

"Well done, Mrs Allen!" hissed Jamie while they waited for his return, and was pleased to see his mother smile. Funny, he thought, when people are kind and sympathetic, she gets sadder and sadder, but as soon as someone treats her unkindly, she comes back fighting.

Mr Claverton came out of his office to greet them. He was a round, smiling, rather pompous little man.

"Ah, Mrs Allen, this is a pleasure. And these are ... er, your two children?" He sounded as though he had not expected children and their hearts sank.

"This is Lucy and this is James, and I have another child, a baby, at home," said Mrs Allen firmly. I might as well tell him the worst and have done with it, she thought.

"Indeed. Well, they do you credit, I'm sure. Now perhaps you will come through to my private office and we will talk about the house."

When they were all seated, he began, "I must confess that although Mr Blunden has been in contact with you about this matter, he unfortunately omitted to mention the fact to me."

The children grew sick with disappointment, but he went on, "He is an old man and in poor health; he is virtually retired. No doubt he got in touch with you feeling that you might accept the post and then ... another bout of illness perhaps, and the matter slipped his mind. So you will bear with me, I hope, if I ask you a few questions and explain again some of the details of the position."

They listened patiently while he told them again about the house and the caretaker's duties. Then he frowned and continued somewhat hesitantly, "You understand, of course, that it is a rather remote house and ... er, for that reason we have had difficulty in finding a caretaker. The last couple we employed stayed only a week ... " He glanced at the children. "They found the isolation too ... " He eyed the children again. Then lowering his voice a tone he said confidentially, "Mrs Allen, I wonder if I might speak with you alone?"

In the outer office Jamie and Lucy sat side by side on straight-backed, slippery leather chairs. Jamie began to kick his heels on the rail but remembered just in time and sighed. Lucy stared at the panelled walls and then turning her head sideways considered the dim portrait above the mantelpiece.

"It's Mr Blunden," she said.

Jamie frowned at it. "So it is," he said, "only he looks a bit younger."

The clerk coughed and looked up with a supercilious smile.

"You are looking at Mr Blunden's portrait?" he asked, with a hint of suppressed amusement in his voice.

"Yes," said Jamie. "He does wear rather odd clothes, doesn't he?"

The young man fairly sniggered with pleasure.

"I'm afraid we've caught you out," he said. "The portrait is in fact of Mr Blunden's great-grandfather who died nearly a hundred years ago."

Jamie and Lucy stared at the painting.

"Oh, but I'm sure that's the man we saw," insisted James. "I'd know him anywhere."

The clerk smiled indulgently. "An understandable mistake. There is a very strong family resemblance. The Blunden nose in particular has been handed down from generation to generation."

Lucy stifled a desire to laugh.

"Yes, indeed," continued the clerk, "if it were not for the clothes, even I could believe that it was the present Mr Blunden."

Jamie considered the clothes: the tight trousers, the waistcoat with lapels, the high old-fashioned collar ... He began to say, "But that's just what he was wearing when ... " but Lucy interrupted hastily.

"Is that the Mr Blunden who was 'struck off'?" she asked, just to change the subject.

The effect on the young man was alarming. He turned very pale and glanced around nervously as if afraid that she might have been overheard.

"S-s-struck off!" he stammered. "What an extraordinary notion. This is a most respectable firm, young lady, and none of its partners has ever been ... " He seemed unable to repeat the terrible words and contented himself with repeating, "a *most* respectable firm!"

"What does it mean anyway?" asked Jamie, who could not see what all the fuss was about.

"It means," said the young man solemnly, "that a lawyer's name is removed from the Roll of Solicitors, that he ceases to be a lawyer because of some offence he has committed. It is not the kind of thing that would happen in a firm like Blunden, Claverton and Smith!"

A likely story, thought Jamie. It's obviously the skeleton in their cupboard and they're afraid it'll get out. Bad for business, I suppose. But to spare the young man any further embarrassment, he only said, "Are you Mr Smith?"

The clerk sighed. "Oh, no," he said, "Mr Smith is the Junior partner. I am Mr Clutterbuck."

"You should be glad," said Jamie comfortingly, and seeing the young man's surprise, he added, "I mean to say, no one could forget a name like that."

Fortunately the door of Mr Claverton's office opened at that moment and the solicitor came out smiling at Mrs Allen.

"Well, dear lady, I must say I am delighted to have a responsible person like yourself to take charge of the house. I shall write to confirm our arrangements and I will contact the estate agent to meet you on your arrival. He will give you the keys and show you everything."

Mrs Allen thanked him and they prepared to leave. As he saw them to the door the lawyer said, "And I feel certain that you will have no trouble from the little matter we spoke of ... Mere country superstition, nothing more ... "

Jamie pricked up his ears.

"Well," said Mrs Allen, as they breathed deeply the cold winter air of the street outside, "I think this calls for a celebration. What shall it be?"

Lucy hesitated, knowing what their father would have offered but unwilling to speak the traditional words.

But Jamie pitched straight in. "Squashy cream cakes at Fortnum's!"

Lucy saw her mother catch her breath and thought, Don't let it all be spoilt.

Mrs Allen sighed. "We haven't had them for a long time, have we?" she said wistfully. Then she smiled. "Oh, well, come on. I've got so skinny lately I shan't even have to diet afterwards."

"Good old Mr Blunden!" said Jamie as they set off along the street.

"Yes," said his mother. "I can't think why he should be so kind to us. An old sick man coming so far to visit us through all that rain."

Lucy was about to say that she didn't think the weather made much difference to him now, but she thought better of it.

Jamie reached for another cream bun and asked, "What was all that about country superstition?"

Mrs Allen, who was just raising her cup to her mouth, replaced it on the saucer with a clatter and said, "Oh, nothing much."

There was an uncomfortable silence and the children waited, knowing that she could never keep a secret.

"It was really nothing," she repeated with even less conviction, "just local gossip."

The children waited.

"Oh, well, I suppose I ought to tell you," she said at last; "you're bound to hear about it in the village. But it was too good a chance to miss and I didn't want you to be frightened.

It's just a lot of nonsense about the house being haunted." She paused anxiously to see their reaction.

"Oh, is that all?" said Jamie, never pausing in the demolition of his bun.

"You don't mind? You don't think you'll be afraid? It's still not too late to change our minds, although it would be a shame. Lucy, dear, what do you think?"

"It's all right," said Lucy calmly. "Old Mr Blunden told us about the ghosts. He said they were nothing to be afraid of." And to herself she added firmly, When the time comes, we shall know what to do.

She was glad that her mother turned away too soon to see her shiver.

Part Two

~~~~~~

3

Lucy sat on the wide stone window-seat in the big drawing-room of the old house. Behind her in the wet April garden the sun was coming out and she felt its warmth touch the back of her neck through the small thick panes of the window.

For three weeks now they had lived in the little cottage that joined the back of the house, and in that time the peace and warmth of the old house had begun to heal them all. The baby's stick-like arms were growing fatter and his pale cheeks had coloured. She and Jamie had begun to lose the sense of some great disaster lurking round the corner, which had haunted them ever since their father's death with its awful legacy of debts and hardship. And their mother had taken the dust-sheets off the grand piano and polished it lovingly, though she had not yet found the courage to touch the silent keys.

Lucy smiled to herself remembering how frightened she had been when they first arrived. The strange way in which they had been brought to the house and the talk of restless ghosts, had preyed upon her mind all through the long journey and she had pictured with growing fear the dark-towered, owl-haunted pile that awaited them. And then to come at last upon this long, low house with the warm grey-brown of its stone walls and its roof patched with lichens in green and gold.

It stood against the sheltering flank of a small hill like a natural outcrop of rock, as if it had grown with the landscape. Beyond its neglected lawns and the weed-filled lake, the woods crowded in, a circle of springing green that seemed not so much to isolate the house as to enclose it in an enchanted circle. They had arrived towards sunset when the lengthening rays of the sun touched all the budding trees and the wide lawns and the warm stone walls with yellow and gold. It seemed the least likely house in all the world to be haunted.

And yet, she thought, there was something strange about it; something that drew her day after day to wander through its rooms. The furniture stood in place under its dust-sheets; the cupboards and drawers were full of old clothes; and little things, workbaskets and books, lay as if waiting patiently to be taken up and for life to begin again.

It was such an old house. It seemed to her sometimes that all the past was gathered up inside it as if in a great box; as though it had a life of its own that continued to exist just beyond the reach of her eyes and ears. And in that way, she thought, it was haunted, although its ghosts were unseen.

She had given up looking for visible ghosts. Once she had asked Mrs Tucker, who came up twice a week to dust and clean, what the stories were that were told in the village. But that stout lady had denied all knowledge of ghosts. "Just a lot of rumours, dearie," she had said firmly, "the sort of tales they tell about any big house that lies empty for a while.

Nothing to be afraid of. After all", she added rather cryptically, "they're only kiddies."

Lucy had repeated this to Jamie.

"Who are?" he demanded.

"Who are what?"

"Only kiddies?"

Lucy considered. "I suppose she means that it is only the village children who say the house is haunted."

"Then it probably is," said Jamie. "Children know a lot more than adults about such things."

But he was only trying to be clever, thought Lucy. As the uneventful weeks had passed, they had both stopped believing in the ghosts, but whereas Jamie was genuinely disappointed, Lucy was secretly relieved.

She had stopped glancing anxiously over her shoulder expecting to see a pale lady in an old-fashioned dress; she no longer started at the sight of a grandfather clock draped in its dust-sheet. She sometimes wondered if they had imagined old Mr Blunden's mysterious hints, or if the old man, who was by all accounts ill, had been wandering in his mind.

And yet ... if the ghosts were not to be seen, she felt sometimes that she could almost hear them. Even now, as she sat in the April sunlight, her ears seemed to catch the faintest sighing of long-ago voices, a dim murmuring as though generations of people were all talking at once but very softly. As she sat listening, her mind drifted and the voices seemed to grow louder, with here and there a word that was clear ... or very nearly so. And then it seemed that the sounds reached her ears from inside, like a roaring in her head that frightened her so that she rose up from the window seat and hurried away, clattering along the stone passage and up the wide staircase until the noise of her feet drove the voices away.

She moved along the first-floor landing and opened the third door on the left. This was her favourite bedroom with a small four-poster bed hung with faded pink curtains. Lucy had always wanted a four-poster bed. She wished that she could sleep in it just once instead of in the little white bedstead in her room in the caretaker's cottage. She opened the dark wooden chest where blankets waited for the bed to be made up again. They still had the faint spicy smell of last year's lavender. I'll ask mother if I can, she thought, just once. But suppose she woke in the night and saw a lady in grey go gliding through the wall? Nonsense, she told herself, there are no such things ... But she closed the door gently as she went out.

She climbed the small twisting stairs where scores of housemaids had come and gone: yawning sleepily in the cold light of dawn as they went down to black the grates; yawning wearily by the light of their candlesticks as they went up again at the end of a long day. High under the roof were their little bedrooms with sloping ceilings, but these had not been used for a long time and they had a forlorn neglected air. Lucy longed to make curtains for the tiny windows, to paste back the wallpaper where it hung down from the walls. She hoped when they found the owners that they would have children to live and play in these little rooms at the top of the house. Whenever the murmuring voices filled her head, it was always the clear, high voices of children that she caught most distinctly.

She pressed her nose to the glass of a window at the back of the house, and beyond the old lead gutter, filled with green moss and the small bones of a long-dead bird, she could just see the courtyard in front of the caretaker's cottage. The red bricks had dried in the sun and Jamie was out there painting a kitchen chair bright blue. He had a lot of newspaper spread about and a large ancient pot of paint which he must have found somewhere. The baby's playpen had been put out in the sun and he bounced up and down calling to Jamie, who snatched his attention from the fascinating painting now and then to call back.

Their voices, echoing in the small room, seemed to Lucy to come from high up around her, sighing through the little attics under the sloping roofs. "Lucy ... Lucy ... Lucy ... " It's the ghosts, she thought, they are calling to me; any moment now they will speak. She panicked as the voice grew louder. "Lucy ... Lucy ... " Then it said, quite distinctly, "Jamie, do you have any idea where Lucy has got to?"

The thudding of her heart died away as she saw her mother standing in the yard. She tapped on the window to draw her attention but it was too far away, so she turned and ran along the passage and down the back stairs, round and round the circling steps, down and down until she arrived, breathless and dizzy, on the ground floor. She plunged through the green-baize door that connected the old house with the cottage, and out panting into the yard.

"Lucy," said her mother, "where have you been?"

"I ... was in ... the attics ... I heard you ... calling."

"Well, darling, it wasn't urgent. You'll break your neck one of these days, racing down those stairs."

"I'm all right," said Lucy, her breath back. "What did you want?"

"I thought it would be nice to have some flowers for the house, to brighten up the place for Easter weekend. There are daffodils in the long grass by the lake, and over in the shrubbery I saw a rhododendron coming into bloom."

"I'll pick some for you."

"Would you, darling? There's an old trug in the back pantry and some kitchen scissors. Oh, and Lucy"—Lucy stopped impatiently in her tracks—"put your wellingtons on; the long grass will be soaking wet after a week of rain."

The wet daffodils shone in a golden heap in the grey trug as Lucy came up the path from the lake. The gravel that crunched beneath her feet was full of sprouting weeds and moss grew in the shady patches. The whole garden was badly neglected but it still had a wild beauty. Now that the summer is coming, thought Lucy, I'll get Jamie to help me tidy it up a bit.

She took a short cut through the overgrown ruins at the east end of the house and stopped to look up at the pointed window arches that stood out like bones against the sky. Like the bones of the bird in the gutter, she thought; all that is left of a long-dead building. She could see that it had once been a wing of the house, but the soaring arches seemed to be of some older style, perhaps some old abbey, destroyed by Henry the Eighth. Clumps of herbs had spread from the garden into the ruins: thyme and marjoram which gave off a sweet, wet scent underfoot. There were wallflowers too, high up on the stonework, and she added to her basket the few that were within reach.

Beyond the ruins, a gravel path wound its way into the shrubbery and she went on in search of the rhododendron. She smelt it before she saw it, a thick, honey scent filling the air, and then round a corner she found the big pale-pink blossoms against dark leaves.

She picked half-a-dozen and then stood idly, breathing in the rich perfume. The air was noisy with birds and she could see through a gap in the bushes the bright green of the lawns with the crowding trees beyond. The heat of the spring sunshine was drying up the heavy rainfall which rose in patches of mist above the grass.

Lucy began to feel strangely drowsy as though the scent of the rhododendron were a sweet, heavy drug. Her mind seemed to be growing still and empty almost as if it had stuck in a groove from which she was unable to move it. Her eyes seemed to focus somewhere short of the point she was looking at. She felt that she ought to make some movement, to break the growing sense of stillness that was creeping over her, but the effort was too great. A blackbird was calling, a single note repeated, a warning note; but she could not turn her head to look at him. It was as if she were concentrating all her mind upon one thing, but against her will and upon something that she did not understand.

Then she sensed that there was something moving through the mist on the lawn, just beyond the point at which her eyes were focused. She could not see very clearly, but it seemed to be two pale figures and they were moving towards her, slowly and with purpose.

Fear gripped her. She dropped the basket and her mind leaped from its groove. She looked wildly around her but there was nothing there. The columns of mist were dissolving above the lawn; the blackbird was singing, a full, bubbling song, as though he might burst at any moment.

Everything was perfectly normal and yet she was afraid. She felt convinced that she had narrowly escaped something. With swift, nervous movements, she gathered up the scattered flowers. Then she ran as fast as she could towards the house only to crash headlong into Jamie who was coming the other way.

"Now then," said Jamie soothingly when he had regained his balance, "what's the matter with you? You look as if you'd just seen a ghost."

Lucy hesitated for a moment before she said, "I thought I had, or rather, two ghosts."

Jamie was delighted. "Where?" he asked. "What were they like? What were they doing?"

Lucy tried to explain but it sounded pretty feeble and Jamie was clearly disappointed.

"Is that all?" he said. "Just the mist over the grass?"

"It wasn't only that ... " Lucy struggled for words. "It wasn't so much what I saw as how I felt: as if something else had taken charge of me. Oh, I can't tell you what it was like but I was frightened. And somehow I was sure that they were ghosts."

She shuddered and, watching her, Jamie was irritated. Why should something interesting like a ghost happen to Lucy, when she only got into a state and ran away? He had

36

been looking for some sign of a white shadowy figure ever since they had come to the house and he hadn't seen a thing yet.

"Now look, Lucy," he said firmly, "if you did see some ghosts, it was a bit mean to run away. After all, we did tell the old man we wouldn't be afraid. He explained all about them needing help. Now let's go back and you can show me where it happened and I'll see if I can see anything."

Lucy had already begun to feel foolish. So, after a moment's hesitation, she took Jamie back along the path until they stood beside the heavy, scented pink blossoms.

"It was just here," she said. "I thought I saw them over there on the lawn."

But everything had changed. The sun was warm and bright and the mist had almost gone. Lucy stood by the bush and watched Jamie as he hunted around for any sign of footprints and grew increasingly scornful when he found none. As if ghosts would leave footprints anyway, she thought crossly.

And then it happened again.

A cloud passed in front of the sun and it was suddenly cold. Lucy became aware of the monotonous single note of the blackbird, the warning call, and again she sensed that her mind was slipping out of her grasp. She heard Jamie chattering as he hunted near by, but she could no longer make out what he was saying. She called his name suddenly, in fear, and reached out her hand to him.

Jamie jumped at her unexpected cry and turning saw his sister's pale frightened face and staring unfocused eyes. Suddenly the whole thing ceased to be a game and he ran to her and took hold of her hand. It was very cold and as he grasped it, he too seemed to be caught in the spell, like the people in the fairy-tale who touched the golden goose.

As they stood motionless, side by side, they became aware of two figures which they sensed rather than saw, passing across the lawn just beyond the line of their vision. Lucy was afraid and clutched at her brother's hand. But Jamie, whose only fear was that she might break the spell, clasped her hand tighter to give her courage. Then they stood without moving until the figures passed into focus: a tall girl in an old-fashioned dress and a little boy, who came walking quite naturally along the path towards them.

4

JAMIE felt distinctly foolish when he saw the children at close quarters. Their clothes were a bit odd it was true: the girl's shabby brown dress was too long and she wore a rather dated straw hat; the boy had narrow white trousers and a blue jacket. But apart from that, he could hardly imagine any two children looking less like ghosts. They must live somewhere near by, he thought, and were dressed in this rather Victorian style by dotty parents. Even Lucy seemed to have lost all nervousness and her hand was quite warm again. He let go of it, feeling that their frozen attitude betrayed too much of their passing fear.

The tall girl looked straight at him with calm grey eyes.

"At last," she said, "we have found someone with a little good sense, who did not run away screaming at the sight of us." She frowned briefly at Lucy.

Lucy lowered her eyes and said apologetically, "I'm awfully sorry, but in the mist I thought for a moment that you were ... ghosts." Then she added by way of justification, "They do say this house is haunted, you know."

The tall girl smiled as if at some private joke. "Yes," she said, "we did know." She looked thoughtful for a moment and then said, "I suppose if I say we *are* ghosts, that you will run away again."

Neither Jamie nor Lucy knew what to make of this. They were beginning to be aware that there was something not quite right about the newcomers, but they could not think what it was.

"I don't believe you are ghosts," said Jamie boldly, "but if you were, we should not be afraid. We know quite a lot about ghosts. They don't do you any harm, in fact they are often people in need of help."

The little boy spoke for the first time. "Who told you that?" he asked.

"An old man we know," Jamie told him, "a lawyer named Mr Blunden."

The little boy kicked the gravel path. "Blundering Blunden," he said contemptuously. "He's a silly old fool! If he had helped us when we asked him ... "

"Oh, don't, Georgie! Please don't say it! It causes him so much grief. You must remember that it's never too late to right a wrong if you are truly sorry."

The little boy snorted and kicked at the gravel again.

Lucy stared at his small foot as it sent the stones flying and then at her own feet. She looked at the girl's feet and then at Jamie's. And then she saw what was wrong.

She said timidly, "You are ghosts, aren't you?"

Jamie stared at her as if she had gone out of her mind.

The tall girl frowned and said, "It all depends upon your point of view. Seen from where you are, I suppose we are in a way. But from where we are, we are not ghosts at all."

Jamie thought this sounded like a lot of rot; but he could see that Lucy knew something.

"What makes you think they are ghosts?" he asked her.

She looked at him nervously and then at the boy and girl. She stepped a little closer to Jamie and said, "They have no shadows."

Jamie looked carefully. The sun was full out now and Lucy's shadow and his own lay clear and black across the pale gravel path. But the other two ... a shiver ran up his spine.

The tall girl was also surveying the ground with interest. "You are quite right," she said in a rather surprised voice. "Look, Georgie, we have no shadows; we must have left them behind."

Georgie looked. He capered about, glancing over his shoulder to see if his shadow was lying behind him. He jumped in the air to see whether it was under his feet. "We haven't, have we, Sara?" he said. He sounded rather pleased as if this put them in a superior position to ordinary people who must walk around with shadows shackled to their ankles.

"But if you are ghosts," said Jamie, "you must be dead, and you don't look very dead."

"Of course we are not dead!" Georgie stopped his prancing and stared up at them. "You do say some stupid things. We are no more dead than you are!"

Sara smiled. "He's really too young to understand," she apologized. "Yet he is right in a way. No one is ever really dead, only dead to certain times and places. To you, the people who lived before you were born are now 'dead', but you are also 'dead' to the people born after you."

"But they haven't been born *yet*," Jamie protested, "and we know we are still alive."

Sara sighed. "I fear it is very hard for you to understand," she said, "but Time is not as you think of it. You think it is a straight line along which you move, so that it is either ahead of you, when you call it the future, or behind you, when you call it the past. But really, it is more like a vast wheel turning and you two and Georgie and I are on different parts of the rim."

Lucy nodded; she thought this sounded quite possible and she felt less afraid.

But to Jamie it sounded like typical girl's reasoning. He decided that there was only one way to find out whether they were ghosts or not, and that was to reach out and touch them. If his hand went right through them... well, at least he would know where he was. When Georgie kicked his feet, the gravel flew, which seemed to suggest that he was pretty solid. And yet, a solid object standing in the way of the sun's rays ought surely to cast a shadow.

As he considered the vast implications of this offence against the laws of nature, Jamie began to be afraid. It was all very well for Lucy to accept a person without a shadow as though it were no more than an unexpected oddity of dress. Lucy lived in a world of books and fairy-tales and was conditioned to take such nonsense in her stride. But Jamie knew better and if the girl and boy had no shadows, then, however lifelike they might appear, there was something very wrong with them.

The story of the headless horror stole back into his mind and as he looked at the girl's hand, he seemed to see the bones inside the skin. If he reached out to touch it, he might find nothing there, which would be bad enough. But suppose his hand grasped a long-dead skeleton and the bones clung to him and the girl began to laugh, a high-pitched, blood-curdling laugh … He shivered and raised his eyes to look at her face, half expecting a skull with glowing eyes in deep-set sockets. Instead he met only the calm, grey eyes which seemed strangely familiar, as though he saw himself in a glass.

Sara smiled. She had seen him shiver; seen his anxious eyes as he stared at her rather thin fingers, and she knew a little of what passed in his mind. She held out her hand to him, slowly and deliberately, like a challenge.

Jamie felt his face redden. His instinct was to grasp her hand, to prove that he was not afraid. And yet the very fact that she seemed to read his thoughts tended only to confirm his worst suspicions.

Lucy put her hand on his arm seeing what he meant to do. She was not afraid to stand and talk with these strangers, but it was another matter for Jamie to touch them. She had not forgotten the sense of helplessness, of being possessed in some way, that had filled her when they first appeared. The girl's face was undeniably pretty but a hundred fairy-tales had convinced Lucy that evil often appears in fair disguises.

Sara and Jamie continued to stare at one another. She was no longer smiling, only waiting, willing him to accept her.

Jamie took a deep breath and summoning all his courage reached out his hand and grasped hers. It was warm and small and very normal.

A great wave of gratitude swept over Sara, and she clasped his hand in both of hers.

"You are the brave one," she said. "Your sister will

understand what is beyond your reach, but you are the one with courage." Her face seemed to grow very sad as she added, "And it is your courage that we desperately need."

In a strange way, once Jamie had taken Sara's hand, the children accepted each other as though their meeting had been perfectly normal. But there remained many questions buzzing in Jamie's mind.

"All this Wheel of Time business," he said, a trifle crossly to hide his embarrassment, "if you're on one bit of the edge and we're on a different bit, how can we possibly be standing here in the same garden at the same time?"

"It was the writing on the window," said Georgie as though that explained everything. "It was in the book," he added, just to make it all crystal clear.

Sara smiled. "It's really rather a long story," she said, "and someone may see us here. Could we not go to the round seat and sit down and I will tell you everything?"

"Where is 'the round seat'?" asked Lucy, puzzled.

Sara looked about her as if to take her bearings. "It used to be over here," she said, and led them away through the dark rhododendrons which grew like trees above their heads. "It has all become sadly overgrown," she observed, "I'm not certain ... " But at that point she darted forward. "Here it is," she called, "but, oh, the view is quite lost."

The round seat was in fact only a semi-circle, a stone seat half-covered with moss in the gloomy shade. The ground about it was paved and a path had once led away from it through a gap in the bushes giving a view down the sloping hillside. Now the bushes had grown up obscuring the view but making a perfect corner for talking undisturbed.

"It all began," Sara told them, "one day when we were alone in the nursery. Georgie was breathing on the window panes and drawing pictures on the misted glass, when suddenly a word appeared already written. It said 'Look', nothing more. We had almost forgotten about it when several days later it happened again, only this time we read 'Look in the library'. At least, that is what we thought it meant to say for the writing was very shaky and the last word ended in a smear as though all had been written with great difficulty. Naturally, we were very much intrigued and took to breathing upon the panes every day until little by little we made out a message that we were to look for a book hidden in the library.

"Unfortunately, this was not easy, for we are forbidden by Mrs Wickens to go into the library ... "

"Yes," interrupted Georgie, "and that awful Meakin is always spying on us and trying to get us into trouble."

Lucy would have liked to ask who these people were, but Sara continued without regarding the interruption.

"However, we watched patiently for a chance and one night, when they were all in bed, we went down to the library and hunted by candlelight until we found, on a high shelf and behind some other books, an old dusty volume. It was written by hand and was full of receipts, remedies and charms which seemed to have been copied from other books. Among them was one called 'A Charm to Move the Wheel of Time'."

Jamie was fascinated. "Did it work?" he asked eagerly. "Oh, I suppose it must have done or you wouldn't be here. Can you teach us the words?"

Sara shook her head. "It isn't as simple as that," she told him. "Be patient a little longer and I'll tell you everything. The book explained that Time is like a great wheel and that at the centre of every wheel, however fast it spins, there is always one point where it is still." She paused for a moment and looked at them inquiringly to see if they would understand.

Jamie was quite good at mechanical problems.

"I suppose, if you accept this Wheel of Time business," he said thoughtfully, "then it would make sense. The two halves of a wheel are always going in opposite directions so where they meet in the centre there would have to be a bit that wasn't moving either way."

"Then you will understand that to go from one part of the Wheel to another, you must pass through the centre where Time is for ever still. To do this takes very great concentration. You must be able to separate your mind completely from the time you are in."

"Well ... yes ... I see that," said Jamie doubtfully, "but I don't see how it can be done."

Sara sighed. "For some," she said, "it is simpler than for others. Little children find it quite easy to forget Time and to lose themselves in make-believe. But as we grow older, the real world takes a hold on us and we can never quite shake it off. But in the old book we found a receipt of herbs. It said that if they were brewed together and the liquid drunk, they would make the mind absolutely still. We hunted through the garden and found all the herbs and we brewed them together over the nursery fire."

"But weren't you afraid to drink it?" asked Lucy. "It might have been poisonous?"

"Oh, I thought of that," said Georgie casually, "so I put some in Mrs Wickens's gin to see if she would die or not."

There was an awkward silence. Jamie and Lucy knew that their disapproval showed in their shocked faces, and Sara looked slightly embarrassed at her brother's bluntness.

"Suppose she had died?" said Lucy timidly.

"Jolly good thing if she did!" said the little boy cheerfully. "She's absolutely beastly!"

"That's all very well," said Jamie, "but if she had died it would have been murder."

"Oh, I don't think so," said Sara quickly. "You see, he didn't give it to her because he thought it was poison but only to make quite sure that it wasn't."

Jamie couldn't help feeling that this argument was unsound.

"It was either Mrs Wickens or the cat," said Sara defensively, "and the cat had never done anyone any harm."

Faced with this choice, Jamie and Lucy saw that any right-minded jury would acquit, and they felt relieved.

"Besides," said Georgie gloomily, "she didn't die at all. She just slept for a long time and woke up next day in a fearful temper saying that she had had terrible dreams. She gets like that from the gin most days," he added.

"Yes," agreed Sara, "only this time she was twice as horrid as usual so we were the ones who suffered most."

Lucy felt very sorry for them.

"The herbs didn't work then?" asked Jamie disappointedly. "You must have been pretty fed up after going to all that trouble."

"Oh, but it couldn't have worked for her," explained Sara patiently. "Georgie only wanted to make sure that it was safe for us to take it. You see it said in the book that the charm will only work on two conditions; the first was 'If the Need for Help is Great Enough' and the second 'If the Will to Help is Strong Enough'."

"But it worked for you," said Lucy, "otherwise you wouldn't be here."

The light faded from the other girl's eyes. "Yes," she said sadly, "it worked for us."

Lucy took hold of her hand as it lay on the cold stone bench.

"Tell us," she said; "tell us what is wrong."

A cool breeze was moving among the dark bushes and the sun had moved so that its rays no longer reached through the tall branches.

Sara stared down at her small shoes.

"For us," she said awkwardly, "the need for help is very great indeed, for unless we can find someone to befriend us, Georgie and I may soon be dead."

5

I T W A S not just the wind springing up and beginning to toss the high branches of the trees that made Jamie and Lucy shiver. It was the growing feeling that they were being drawn into events beyond their comprehension.

Ghosts who appeared from the past, provided that they came in such acceptable form, with no more frightening strangeness than a shadow more or less, had something of the fascination of men from Mars. Jamie had read stories of people who encountered beings from outer space and held conversations about life on other planets. But none of the unearthly visitors had ever talked about their personal problems.

Lucy had begun to feel that she was watching a play where the audience, in accordance with the rules of plays, could not intervene, but in which the characters were real.

She said anxiously, "Surely you don't mean that someone is planning to harm you?"

"It's our uncle," said Georgie angrily. "He's plotting to get rid of us. But he won't get me! Why, I'd have finished him off long ago if Sara hadn't ... "

"Oh, Georgie," said Sara patiently, "you know there is nothing we can do. Besides, it isn't Uncle Bertie, he's not really bad ... "

Now there's a Wicked Uncle, thought Jamie; all the best stories have one. I've been eating rich food and reading too late at night: I shall wake up soon.

"Tell us from the beginning," said Lucy, and Jamie half expected Sara to start "Once upon a time".

But she said, "Our grandfather had two sons who were half-brothers. Our father was the elder but he and our mother died three years ago when their carriage overturned."

A car-crash, thought Jamie, she means a Victorian car-crash; only they lost both parents. If Mother had gone with him to New York ... A wave of desolation swept over him and it no longer seemed like a dream or a story.

"After they died ... " Sara was trying to tell her story matter-of-factly but the trembling of her voice gave her away. "After they died," she repeated more firmly, "Uncle Albert became our guardian. We seldom saw him at first. He left us here with our governess because he found life in London much gayer. He was very young, you see, and was easily led once he fell into bad company.

"But his gay life lasted only as long as his share of our grandfather's money. It wasn't a great fortune for he was only a younger son. Most of the money had passed to Papa and then to Georgie, though it is held in trust until he is of age. After a while, Uncle Bertie began to fall into debt but he would not change his ways and his money melted until he had barely enough to live on.

"He started to come down and live with us for a few weeks at a time to save some money and escape his creditors. Then he would suddenly declare that he could not stand the dullness of the country a day longer, and he would hurry back to London."

"And half the silver cutlery with him," added Georgie.

"We cannot be certain," said Sara. "It could have been one of the servants. He is not bad, only foolish." She seemed almost to plead for him, and Lucy saw that she had been very fond of her gay, young uncle.

"The trouble began on one of his trips to London. He went to the music-hall one night and fell hopelessly in love with one of the ballet girls. Her name is Arabella and she is very pretty, but in her mind she is only a child. She cares for nothing but clothes and sweet things, although she is not really bad at heart."

"Oh, really, Sara!" her brother wrinkled his nose in distaste. "The way you tell it, absolutely everyone is good inside. Next you will find some hidden virtue in old Mrs Wickens."

Sara's face clouded. "Mrs Wickens is an evil old woman," she said, "and her husband is a brute. You see," she explained, "they are Arabella's parents and, with our uncle, they have all come to live at the house.

"The old lady used to run a gin-palace. She is coarse and mean and quite unscrupulous. Her husband was once a prize-fighter but the boxing damaged his brain, I fear, for he is little more than a mindless mountain, and does whatever his wife tells him."

"When he is not too drunk to move," put in Georgie crossly.

Lucy was appalled. "But how can your uncle bear to have them in the house?" she exclaimed.

"Oh, he thinks of nothing but Bella." Sara sighed. "He wants to marry her, you see, but she is only seventeen and cannot marry without her parents' consent. Mrs Wickens is not going to waste her daughter on a penniless younger son and she pesters him all the time saying what a shame it is that the money must go to Georgie.

"One day we heard her remarking cheerfully upon how thin we were looking and it was true for she had taken over the housekeeping and we were getting very little to eat. But Georgie became very skilful at climbing through the pantry window ... "

"It's jolly difficult," he interrupted, "I doubt if anyone else could do it. I'll wager Tom could not!"

"I'm sure he couldn't," said Sara soothingly; "but you must let me finish my story, for time is short."

Her brother tossed his head impatiently and she went on, "Mrs Wickens found, much to her annoyance, that starving us was a slow business, so she took away most of our blankets and insisted that we sleep with all the windows wide open, even on the coldest nights. But Tom told us to put old newspapers between the blankets, which proved to be very warm. And somehow the fresh air, though it is said to be very unwholesome, seemed to keep us in excellent health while the others, who slept with roaring fires and the windows safely closed, fell victims to one ailment after another."

Jamie and Lucy thought this hardly surprising but it did not seem the moment for a lecture on modern advances in hygiene.

"For a long time", continued Sara, "we treated the whole affair as a battle of wits and did not truly think ourselves in danger. But then we overheard Mrs Wickens and her husband discussing the possibility of an accident befalling us. We were alarmed at this since an accident is hard to foresee and harder to guard against. We went to Uncle Bertie but he was sitting with Bella and he told us to be off and not to bother him. It was then that we decided to write to our other guardian for help."

"Who is your other guardian?" asked Lucy, who had a strange feeling that she knew the answer.

"He is one of the family solicitors," Sara told her, "a man named Frederick Blunden."

Lucy was about to point out that she and Jamie had met him, when she realized how foolish it would sound. Their Mr Blunden must surely be the grandson of Sara's guardian. And yet she wondered ... But she only said, "Was he very shocked when he found out what was happening?"

Sara smiled sadly. "Who can tell?" she said, "for he never answered our letter."

"Maybe it didn't reach him," said Jamie. "Did you post it yourself?"

"No," she admitted, "but Tom took it and he promised that it was safely dispatched."

Before Lucy could ask who Tom was, Georgie burst in, "Of course old Blunden got it, but he thinks only of his fees. He would not dare to challenge our uncle. Wait until I inherit," he said darkly, "I shall throw him out on his ear! I shan't forget the way he has treated us."

The others were silent. They could see that his future vengeance counted for little unless he could survive the present danger.

"Couldn't you run away?" suggested Jamie at last.

"We did," said Georgie gloomily, "but they caught us in the village and we were taken back. Mrs Wickens shut us in the cellar for days and fed us on bread and water for a week."

"But is there no one you can trust?" asked Lucy. "You said you had a governess."

"Oh, she went long ago, soon after the Wickenses arrived." Sara sighed. "She said she was a decent woman and would not stay in the house with them. I can't blame her, for they treated her with great disrespect. And when Mrs Wickens took over the housekeeping, the servants began to go. Some gave warning and left because they would not tolerate her rudeness; others, like cook and our old nanny, protested when she was harsh to us and were promptly dismissed. One by one, all the servants were replaced by others brought down from London, most of them creatures who would not get a post in any decent household.

"There is no one in the house we can trust and the estate is so vast that we rarely see anyone from outside. The only friend we have left is Tom, the gardener's boy, who lives in the lodge cottage a long way from the house. His father is a surly old man, but Tom would do anything he could to help us."

"But what can he do?" said Georgie scornfully. "Tom Fletcher is only a servant after all, and they are not very intelligent."

Sara coloured angrily. "Georgie! How can you be so mean! Tom is as clever as you or I."

Georgie sulked. "He can't even read," he said stubbornly.

"Of course he cannot! He has never had the opportunity. But I am teaching him and he learns very quickly. If you had had to learn to read at the end of a long day's work in the garden, you would never have gone beyond 'A'!"

"He is not cleverer than I am!" Georgie raised his voice and Lucy saw that he was jealous.

Sara seemed to see it too, for she smiled at him suddenly and said, "Georgie dear, of course he is not. But he is our friend, the only one we have, and I will not have you be unkind to him."

For a moment the child continued to scowl as if bent on punishing his sister. But the desire to be friends with her was too strong so he stopped kicking the stone bench and grinned at her.

Lucy marvelled to herself that she could have mistaken him for a ghost. He was such an ordinary little boy with his moods and his tantrums. He might do for one of those spirits who throw china and play tricks, she thought, but they are always invisible and this child was very solid-looking.

"But surely," Jamie was saying, "surely there is something you can do?" but his voice lacked conviction.

"We have done the only thing we could," said Sara. "It was after we tried to run away that the writing began on the nursery window. It seemed to us that someone was trying to help us, so we sought out the book and made the potion. We resolved that if we could not run to another place for help, we would go to another time."

At once Jamie understood everything, or thought he did.

"But of course!" he said eagerly. "You can stay here, in

our time, where they can never reach you." He swung round to Lucy. "They can live with us!" he exclaimed delightedly. "I don't know quite how Mother will take it, she may find it hard to understand at first, but once she knows they are in danger ... " He turned back to Sara. "I'm afraid we're pretty hard up," he said apologetically, "and with two more to feed you may find the meals a bit plain, but you can share Lucy's room and ... " His voice trailed away as he saw that she was trying not to cry. "Oh Lord," he said awkwardly, "I didn't mean to upset you. Whatever did I say?"

"It is only because you are so kind." Sara sniffed, and accepted Lucy's proffered handkerchief. "I had forgotten that people could be kind. Oh, I wish we could just walk home with you as you say, and never, never see Mrs Wickens again. But it is not so simple. You see, after a time, we begin to feel thin and light-headed; then everything fades around us and we are back in our own time again."

"And we always arrive back at exactly the same time as we left," added Georgie, "so that it is no use to take it to pass the time when we are shut in the cellar all day."

"But if you can't stay in our time, what good was it to come?" Jamie was at a loss, but Lucy was beginning to understand.

"You want us to help?" she asked Sara, knowing as she said it that they would be committed, that they were starting along a path from which there would be no turning back.

"It is our only hope." Sara's voice was apologetic. "We have tried several times before but either the gardens were deserted or, if we saw someone, they could not see us, or, if they could see us, they screamed and ran away."

Lucy wished she had been braver.

"It was as though we were trapped," the other girl continued, "trapped behind a wall we could not see, through which we cried for help and were not heard. Until your brother came, and he was not afraid."

"But what can we do?" asked Jamie, who could not bear to see anything in a cage.

"You want us to go back with you?" said Lucy. It was not really a question for she already knew and did not want to know.

Sara nodded.

"Go with you? You mean back to your time?" Jamie could hardly believe his good fortune. "But is it possible? I mean, how can we?"

"I will help you to find the herbs," said Sara. "Most of them seem to be here still, growing wild about the garden. You can brew the potion as we did. After that, it depends upon whether 'the Will to Help is Great Enough'."

"Well, it is," said Jamie who found it a bit embarrassing when Sara was so solemn. "You don't think we would stand around and let that awful old woman do you in. Why I'd ... "

"Sara! Sara!" Georgie's voice, high and anxious, cut across Jamie's words.

They all turned to look at him and saw that he had grown very pale, his skin almost transparent. "I don't feel well," he said miserably.

At once, Sara was on her knees beside him. "Don't be

afraid," she said calmly. "Remember that when you get back, I shall be there. You were very brave when it happened before. It is soon over and … "

Even as she spoke, with her arm around him, he grew thin and faint and was suddenly gone.

Lucy felt sick. One minute he had been there, so real and solid, and the next … only the empty air, the waving bushes behind him, the marks of his feet on the gravel path. All this would happen to her and to Jamie: and how could they be certain that they would ever return?

Even Jamie was startled.

Sara rose to her feet and dusted off her dress. "It is because he is so young," she said matter-of-factly. "I am afraid to let him drink too much and so he returns before me. But since no time passes while we are away, we always arrive back together."

Jamie swallowed hard. "How can we be sure," he asked, "that, if we do drink the potion, we shall go back to your time? We might go forward as you do, or we might go back to a different time."

"I must confess that I do not know for certain." Sara frowned. "It seems to me that if you are meant to help us … and perhaps if we hold hands as we go … But I cannot be sure. Perhaps you should not take the risk."

"We'll chance it," said Jamie firmly. "I think you're probably right about holding hands."

"I'll help you to find the herbs," said Sara. "Georgie is a warning to us that I may soon follow him, so I must search for them before I begin to grow weak."

As she hurried away along the gravel path, her small feet

in their white stockings seemed hardly to touch the ground.

"They will probably be near the old herb garden," she called back over her shoulder. Her full skirts were flurried by the wind as she ran, and the ribbons on her flat straw hat streamed out behind her.

Jamie could not bear to see her go. He seized Lucy's hand and they hurried after her.

She paused by the old sundial and began to hunt about among the overgrown plants that surrounded it. They heard her say, "Balm and hyssop, madwort and musk ... " as she picked a sprig here, a few leaves there. She muttered to herself as she searched for others and found them with little cries of triumph. At one point she paused in her bird-like darting and, gazing at the bunch of herbs in her hand, said anxiously, "Oh, I do hope I've got it right!"

Not half as much as I do, thought Lucy. I've got to drink the wretched brew. She particularly disliked the sound of 'madwort'.

"Toad flax ... and bergamot!" Sara made a last dive into a clump of russety-green leaves, and stood up looking very pleased with herself.

"Here," she said, holding out her hand with a bunch of herbs. "Put five leaves of each into a bowl, mind it is not metal, and pour on hot water but do not let it boil. Keep it warm for about an hour, and then strain off the liquid through a piece of woollen cloth." She spoke quickly so that it was all they could do to follow, and even as they watched, she was growing pale.

"Bring the potion and meet me here at ten o'clock tomorrow morning."

"All right," said Jamie eagerly but Lucy, remembering just in time, said, "It will be Good Friday: Mother will want us to go to church with her in the morning."

"The evening then!" Sara's voice was anxious and her face had taken on that transparent lightness. "Here ... by the sundial ... an hour before sunset ... "

She was growing wraithlike and then, at the last moment, she stretched out her hands in a pleading gesture and cried, "Promise you will not fail us ... " Then she was gone.

Jamie stood staring at the place where she had been, and Lucy heard him say under his breath, "I promise!"

6

"WE must not think of our Good Friday worship as a memorial service, but rather as the celebration of a great victory ... "

Lucy shifted uncomfortably in the straight-backed pew. The wooden seat had been polished to a high gloss by generations of fidgety worshippers, and as her feet did not quite reach the ground, she kept slipping forward. She wondered if it would help to edge the hassock towards her with her toe and use it as a footrest. But on reflection she decided that her shoes were too muddy from the walk across the fields and that it would be foolish to put mud on the dingy plush where she would shortly have to kneel.

She tried hard to concentrate upon what the vicar was saying, but to do this she needed to keep her eyes on his earnest face, and every time she slid slowly forward in her seat, he vanished out of sight behind a large pink hat with much veiling.

Lucy wondered about the potion. The brewing had been fairly simple. They had counted the right number of leaves into a small ovenglass jug, and Jamie had put on the kettle and added the hot water in the kitchen under cover of making everyone a nice cup of tea. But the brew, when it was finished, looked, in Jamie's phrase, "a bit grotty", and Lucy didn't like the thought of drinking it.

"Let us resolve that in us this day shall die all the uncharitable thoughts, the corrosive indifference, the acts of selfishness, that come between us and the love of God ... "

Lucy heaved herself back in her seat and stared at the vicar. With his head emerging above the pink spotted tulle he seemed, ridiculously, to be wearing a ladies evening dress, and she stifled a desire to giggle. It was a kind face, though, she thought, and he looked as if he meant what he was saying. He was quite young and seemed the sort of person you could go to with your problems. Lucy felt tempted to ask him what they should do about Sara and Georgie. But she knew that once she had explained that it was all happening a hundred years ago, it would be hard to get anyone over the age of sixteen to consider the problem seriously.

There was something about the whole business that was worrying her, but she kept pulling her mind away when it tried to consider the matter. It was rather like having a bad tooth, she thought; your tongue keeps poking it to see if it hurts but not very hard for fear of starting a pain you can't stop. Gingerly, she let her mind drift into the problem: if something was happening a hundred years ago, then it had already happened, and however much you cared nothing could change it. So, if Sara and Georgie were going to die, then they were already ... The pain of thinking became too sharp and she swung her thoughts back to what the vicar was saying.

"... and of the Holy Ghost, Amen."

He had finished his sermon and was coming down from the pulpit.

Gratefully, Lucy sprang to her feet in the general surge of people and reached for her hymn-book.

"Through the night of doubt and sorrow
Onward goes the pilgrim band,"

Jamie always enjoyed the hymns most of all. Lucy had accused him of being tone-deaf and out-of-tune, but he did not believe a word of it. To him it seemed that his voice rang clear as a bell, and he sang with great gusto. If the people in front turned round to stare at him, as they so often did, he assumed that they wanted to see who could be the owner of such a rich, tuneful voice, and he smiled so engagingly that even music-lovers had been known to smile back.

"Chasing far the gloom and terror,
Brightening all the path we tread."

Today the hymns were particularly welcome. They took his mind off the nagging doubt which he dared not share with Lucy, but which had distracted him all through the service.

He knew he was not very bright in some ways. His mind

never made sudden, brilliant darts of understanding as Lucy's did. All that business about Time being circular, which Lucy found quite simple, seemed to him a picturesque piece of fantasy. As an explanation of how Sara and Georgie came to be walking around their garden a hundred years out of time, it sounded pretty thin. But he had held Sara's hand, so his common sense told him she was really there; and he had watched her vanish with his own eyes, so he believed her story about drinking the potion. He even believed that when he and Lucy drank it, they would end up in some other time, though he was not at all sure it would be Sara's.

The point at which his common sense baulked and refused to go along was at the suggestion that if he and Lucy did find themselves face to face with the formidable Mrs Wickens, they would be able to do anything to frustrate her schemes. After all, he thought, the past is the past and you can't get away from it. What's done is done. If only I knew what did happen.

He sighed and then, taking a deep breath, threw himself headlong into the last verse of the hymn.

"Soon shall come the great awakening,
Soon the rending of the tomb ... "

He always liked the bit about the great awakening. He could see in his mind's eye the sleepers in the churchyard, sitting up and yawning and rubbing their eyes, with the green turf folded back like a blanket and the jars of daffodils overturned.

And then, as he listened admiringly to his own rich

rendering of the familiar words, a light came on in Jamie's mind. "The rending of the tomb". Of course, it would all be there, written down for them to read, carved into solid stone. For once he would dazzle Lucy with his cleverness.

He raised his voice gratefully, and sang the 'Amen' louder than ever.

The vicar smiled politely at Mrs Monk-Burton with her heavily powdered face under her unsuitable pink net hat and tried not to think uncharitable thoughts. But it was not easy, for he knew her to be a selfish and vain old woman. He shook her hand and tried to look modest and grateful as she announced in her loud, patronizing voice, "Such a splendid sermon, Vicar. Just what I am always saying myself, all that about sacrificing ourselves for others. Isn't that what I'm always saying, Horace?" and she poked her elbow into the thin nervous-looking man who stood beside her.

"Oh, always, dear, always," he said eagerly. "Yes, indeed, all the time."

His wife frowned at him for a moment as though suspecting sarcasm, but seeing only anxious agreement, she turned back to the vicar.

"We must bear one another's burdens," she said with a heavy sigh, "how true, how true!"

The vicar smiled briefly and turned to greet his next parishioner.

But when he saw that it was the young widow who had taken the caretaker's cottage at the Old House, and that she had three children with her, including a rather fretful baby, he decided that Mrs Monk-Burton might be of use for once.

He guessed from their muddy shoes that the young family had come by the field path, but even by that route the Old House was two miles from the village. No buses ran in that direction, and it was a long way to walk carrying a child.

He smiled and greeted her, tried without success to make the baby laugh, and seeing that the Monk-Burtons had almost reached their glossy car, he called them back.

"Dear Mrs Monk-Burton," he said, "knowing how you love to be of service, I have no hesitation in asking you to give Mrs Allen and her family a lift."

She frowned. "I'm afraid we're not going that way ... " she began.

"Which way are you going?" asked the vicar sweetly.

"Well, we have to go by the Furniston road," she said, choosing the only road that crossed the high heath and passed through no villages.

"Perfect! Then you could drop them all at the gates of the Old House."

"The Old House? I didn't know there was anyone living there. Oh, very well!" She conceded defeat as ungraciously as possible, but Mr Monk-Burton seemed delighted as he shepherded his small party towards the big car.

The vicar smiled as he watched them go and, with a positively unchristian feeling of triumph, went off to have his lunch.

As they drew near the car Jamie, who saw the vicar's well-meant manœuvres ruining his plan, said to his mother,

"I say, would you mind if Lucy and I walked back the way we came? I saw some nests I'd like to have a look at, and there wasn't time on the way here."

Before she could answer, Mrs Monk-Burton, seeing a chance to reduce the number of muddy feet in her car by four, said quickly,

"But of course; so much healthier for the dear children to walk, and so pleasant to see the dear birds."

Jamie smiled at his mother. "May we," he asked, "if we promise not to be too long?"

"All right," she said, "and by the time you get back I'll have fed the baby and the lunch will be ready."

He gave her a grateful peck of a kiss and seizing Lucy by the hand dragged her back across the churchyard towards the footpath gate on the far side.

Lucy protested crossly. "I want to go with Mummy," she said, "I don't care a bit about the 'dear birds'!" She had been quite taken with the idea of herself riding in the big, glossy car.

"Listen," said Jamie, "that wasn't really why I wanted to walk. While we were in church I had a brilliant idea. All we have to do is to hunt around in the churchyard and look at the names on the graves. If we find two graves with ... " he checked himself, sensing that Lucy would find the idea of the children's graves too ghoulish. He rephrased the sentence, "I mean, once we have made sure that none of the gravestones has Sara and Georgie's names on, then we shall know that they didn't die." He paused and looked at Lucy for encouragement, but her face was wary and thoughtful.

"Don't you see?" he persisted; "we shall know in advance that we managed to save them, and then we can go off into the past knowing that it will be all right."

Lucy, hearing his eager tones, felt a bit churlish that she

could not share his enthusiasm. She did not like to pour cold water on his ideas because he did not have them very often, but there was something about the whole scheme that gave her the shivers.

"We couldn't be sure," she said. "They might have buried them secretly; people often do when they've murdered someone." Even saying the words made her feel queer. She had accepted that Sara and Georgie, coming from a different time, were in a way already dead, but to think of someone actually ... She shook the thought out of her mind.

Jamie was saying cheerfully, "But of course they wouldn't. If their uncle wants to inherit the money, it would be no use having them just disappear. What he would have to do would be to make it look like an accident. Then he would bury them in the churchyard and pretend to be very sad and all that."

"I don't like it," said Lucy abruptly. "It's a silly idea. I don't think it's nice and I shan't look."

"All right, don't!" Jamie went into a huff. It was just like Lucy: she was always the one who had the bright ideas and he had to help her carry them out. She seemed to think he was some kind of beast of burden. Now that he had come up with a brilliant idea, she called it silly just because she had not thought of it first. "I can look by myself," he said moving off along the line of gravestones. "And I shan't tell you if it's there or not!" he called over his shoulder.

Lucy had gone off in the other direction and, with her back towards him, she was swinging gently on the kissing-gate that led to the footpath.

When she heard his sudden shocked cry of, "Lucy, Lucy,

come here!" her heart sank. She felt she had known all along that this would happen. She climbed down sadly and went to stand beside him.

He was staring down at the inscription on a small, grey, time-worn stone. Lucy read the names:

SARA CATHERINE LATIMER
GEORGE RICHARD LATIMER

and the date below.

"It's tomorrow," said Jamie, his voice dull with disbelief. "It's tomorrow, only a hundred years ago!"

Lucy could think of nothing comforting to say but she took hold of his hand.

They both started violently as a voice from behind them said,

"Ah, that's right, a hundred years ago, poor little things. 'Twas a real tragedy and 'tis no wonder if they wanders around the garden still, poor little lost souls!"

They turned, half expecting another ghost, only to find a short, sturdy old man, with a friendly face under a battered brown hat. He gave off a strong smell of tobacco and onions that was reassuringly human.

"Why, I'm sorry if I startled 'ee then, my dears," he went on, seeing their pale faces. "I thought 'ee'd 'ave 'eard me comin' on the gravel like. Just lookin' at the grave of them poor kiddies, eh? Sad business, very sad."

"Do you know who they were, then?" asked James, half unwilling to pry any further but feeling that nothing could be worse than what they already knew.

"Ah," the old man nodded, "I reckon I could tell 'ee about every little grave in this churchyard. I bin sexton 'ere more than forty years afore the diggin' got too much for me. Not that I'm past a bit of diggin' mind yer; I still does me old garden single-'anded an' I sees the churchyard's kept tidy, but 'tis the depth as gets 'ee. Six feet deep, y'see," he explained confidentially, "an' when you'm gettin' to the bottom 'tis too far to throw the dirt up. Not to mention the trouble gettin' out when you'm finished. 'One of these days you won't get out again, Benson,' the vicar says to me. 'Tha's true enough,' I tells 'im, 'for it comes to all of us, but I ain't ready for it quite yet!' "

He laughed cheerfully but Lucy was in no mood for graveyard humour. Horrid old man, she thought. She turned her eyes away and stared at the next gravestone. It seemed to be very old, with a carved death's head like a grinning monkey.

Jamie pointed to Sara and Georgie's grave. "Tell us about them," he said.

"About they poor children?" The old man's voice grew sentimental again. "Ah, 'twas a dreadful thing! A fire it was, one night, an' them fast asleep in their little beds. By the time the flames was spotted, 'twas already burning like a furnace, for it started in the library, they say, an' the books burned like tinder. No one could get to them, poor little mites. Not that they didn't try, mind. Down in the corner of the churchyard there," he pointed towards a clump of trees, "you'll find a little grave with no stone, but 'tis always covered with violets an' forget-me-nots in season. They say 'twas the little gardener's boy as tried to save them. My old grandfather used to tell me the story when I was as young as you are now, about 'ow this little lad climbed up the drain-pipe to their bedroom window. But somehow the pipe gave way, I suppose 'twas the heat on the lead, or mebbe it weren't properly fastened, an' just as 'ee reached the window, the poor little lad come plungin' down an' was killed.

"An' then there was their guardian too. 'Ee'd bin to the 'ouse that day an' was on 'is way back to London when 'is carriage broke down. When 'ee saw the flames in the distance, 'ee seized a 'orse an' come ridin' back as if the devil 'imself was at 'is 'eels. My grandad 'eard it all from the lodge-keeper at the 'ouse, and 'ee said as 'ow the old man took on somethin' cruel when 'ee knew they was dead. 'Too late!' 'ee kept saying with the tears runnin' down 'is face, and then 'My fault, all my fault!' though what could 'ee 'ave done, poor gentleman? An' then, all of a sudden, 'ee collapsed in a 'eap and they 'ad to carry 'im away. Some said as 'ow 'ee died of grief and others that 'ee was never right in 'is 'ead again. And there's some claims to 'ave seen 'is ghost too, wanderin' about the Old 'Ouse, besides them poor little ghosts of children that comes and goes in the gardens."

"Have other people ... I mean, have people really seen them?" asked Jamie.

"Oh, indeed they 'ave!" said the old man eagerly. "Why, the couple as used to live in the caretaker's cottage, they saw 'em twice, little misty white figures, walkin' across the lawn. They wouldn' stay; packed their bags an' went back where they came from. Ah, 'tis 'aunted sure enough! You don't want to go near the Old 'Ouse, I'm tellin' 'ee. Why, none of the village folks ... "

"We live there," said Lucy rather frostily.

The old man's face registered surprise, regret, and false jollity, all in rapid succession.

"Why then, I was only kiddin' you," he said with a wheezing chuckle. "Ho-ho-ho! Made it all up I did. I knows 'ow kiddies loves to 'ear a story. Mind you, there's no such things as ghosts!"

"That depends on your point of view," said Lucy, "but you needn't worry, we're not afraid of them."

The old sexton gazed at her uncomfortably.

Jamie thought he was rather nice and that Lucy was being a bit acid. After all, the old man couldn't possibly know that he was talking about their friends. And it was best to know what had happened, however depressing it might be.

"Well, thanks for telling us the story," he said. "It was very interesting, but we have to hurry off home now, or we shall be late for lunch."

He smiled at the sexton who said "Goodbye" rather awkwardly, and then taking Lucy's arm, he hurried her out of the churchyard, through the kissing-gate, and along the path towards home.

They had gone quite a way before Jamie realized that Lucy was crying. There was no sound, but fat tears rolled in a steady stream down her cheeks.

"Oh, Lucy," he said, "Lucy, don't get upset."

"I ... can't ... help ... it ... " she said between stifled sobs. "I keep thinking about Sara and that little boy ... "

Jamie walked along in silence. He knew she was waiting

for him to say something, but it was hard to think of anything comforting.

After a while, Lucy said, "Do we have to go, Jamie? Do we have to drink that awful stuff and ... "

"We can't very well let them down," he said.

"But I couldn't bear to be there and see it all happen if there's nothing we can do to stop it. It would be too awful!"

"I know," he agreed miserably, "but ... well ... I don't think you should abandon a cause just because it's hopeless. We must go, Lucy, at least, I mean *I* must. You see I promised ... "

"But if there is no way?"

"I know, but I did promise. You didn't make any promises, Lucy; you needn't come if you don't want to."

"Oh, of course I shall come if you are going." Lucy said it crossly to hide her concern for him.

They walked on along the narrow path which led through a wood where brilliant leaves burst from tree-buds overhead and folded yellow daffodils opened in a bright carpet along the ground. It was very different from the grey littered pavements of Camden Town and, looking about her, Lucy felt her spirits rise in spite of everything. It is hard not to be hopeful in the woods in April.

"Don't you think it just might be possible to do something?" she asked wistfully.

"To save them? No, how could we? What is past is past. You can't undo it, you can only change the future." Jamie would have liked to say 'Yes', but he knew that it was crueller to raise her hopes and then dash them, so he spoke bluntly.

"But Sara said that our future is the past to people who

come after us, and we can change that. After all, this is the future for Sara and Georgie and if we are in their time ... "

"It isn't possible," said Jamie doggedly. He could not make head or tail of Sara and Lucy when they started juggling with words, but his common sense told him what was possible and what was not.

Lucy said, "If someone had asked you yesterday whether you could travel through time, would you have said that was impossible?"

Jamie saw that she was making a trap for him to fall into. "I suppose I might have done," he said cautiously, looking for a way round it.

"There you are then: anything is *possible*."

But the trap was empty. "I shan't believe it is possible", said Jamie, "until *we* have done it."

"But Sara said ... "

"What Sara said is not evidence, it's hearsay," said Jamie smugly. He remembered this from a court scene in a television series.

Lucy was furious at finding herself outwitted, and sulked the rest of the way home.

Jamie was sorry when the first flush of triumph had worn off and he thought he would butter her up a bit. But then he decided that she was better off sulking than weeping, and he watched her with a fond smile as she stalked along ahead of him. Good old Lucy. He knew that she would insist on going with him, whatever might lie ahead, and he was glad in a way. It would be bad enough as it was, but worse, somehow, to face it alone, the one helpless onlooker. He wished he did not have to go, but he felt bound by his promise.

Besides, he couldn't leave them alone if there was anything he could do to help. And yet, what could he do? He turned his face up to the blue sky that shone through the green tracery of branches, and racked his brains for an answer. But the only possible answer came from his heart: I might comfort them, I suppose.

7

JAMIE heaved a deep sigh and asked, "Lucy, are you quite sure you want to come?"

"Yes, yes, yes! I've told you a hundred times!" Lucy's voice was irritable with misery. "I do wish you would stop asking."

"Well, I wish you would stop grizzling!" said Jamie reasonably. "You say you want to go on with it, and then you sit there sniffing and snuffling all the time. Sara and Georgie may be here at any minute" – he glanced at his watch – "they should have been here twenty minutes ago, and what will they think if they see you crying? They'll want to know why, and I'm not going to tell them. I mean, how can you tell someone they are going to ... " He couldn't face the end of the sentence, but Lucy understood.

"I'm sorry." She sniffed again and, fumbling out her handkerchief, blew her nose and tried to pull herself together.

There was a long silence and then she said, "Maybe they won't come. Maybe we imagined the whole thing." She began to sound hopeful. "It could have been a sort of hallucination."

Jamie considered the idea and found it half comforting and half disappointing. "I hope it was," he said. But he had taken Sara's hand and he knew that she had been real.

"Why do you hope I'm a hallucination?" Sara's voice was gentle and amused but both the children jumped, partly with surprise and partly with embarrassment. She was standing beside the sundial, looking down at them, and she was alone.

Jamie got to his feet awkwardly and tried to change the subject. "Hello," he said, "we were just wondering where you had got to. Where is Georgie?"

"I'm afraid he is locked in the cellar. That is really why I am so late. He had a slight disagreement with Mrs Wickens and I fear he was very rude to her." She smiled suddenly and went on, "It was wrong, of course, but I cannot pretend I was not glad. She was so put out, I thought she would have a fit of some kind; but she just screamed at one of the servants to lock him in the cellar, and went off in search of her bottle."

"But will he be all right?" asked Lucy anxiously. "Do you think it was safe to leave him?"

"Well, I was afraid to do so at first," Sara told her. "I fetched Tom and we tried to get him out by the coal chute, but it wasn't possible. We talked to him and he sounded quite happy, but it seemed wrong to go until I remembered that no time would pass while I was away.

"So I left Tom on guard beside the cellar grating and drank the potion. But I have taken only a little for I am too anxious to stay here for long. I feel safer always when we are together. Georgie is reckless but he is only a child and I know they are plotting some evil thing against us."

Lucy turned pale. It had been bad enough to think of the fire happening to someone far away in another time; but with Sara standing there, so close and so real, the breeze lifting the long, dark strands of her hair ... However much she tried, the tears began again.

"Oh, Lucy, don't," said Jamie, sitting down beside her, "please don't, not *now*."

Sara stood staring at them. Then she said, "There is something you know. Please tell me."

Lucy's tears flowed faster than ever and Jamie was in despair.

"It's nothing, nothing," he repeated, feeling a terrible fool.

"You must tell me." Sara's voice was kind but firm. "Whatever it is, you *must* tell me."

Jamie looked up and saw that she was very calm. "Well," he began, "well, you see ... " but he couldn't find the words.

"Don't be afraid to say it. I know much more than you think I do. We did not want to tell you too much, in case you were afraid."

"It was in the graveyard," Jamie blurted out the truth, "on the tombstone. We found your name and his. The sexton said it was a fire." He glanced away. Even now, he could not say that it would be tomorrow.

There was a silence and when he looked up again, he was surprised to find that she did not look particularly distressed. Only her face was very sad.

The sun was setting and as it went, a few horizontal beams escaped from the clouds and lit up her face with a strange radiance.

"It is true," she said, "it was a fire."

Lucy seemed to see the flames flickering across her face, but she could not look away.

"I know about the grave," Sara went on, "I too have

walked in the churchyard, but Georgie doesn't know. He is brave but very young: we could not tell him everything. We could not tell him that it will be tomorrow."

She hesitated for a moment and Jamie wondered whom she meant when she said 'we'.

But she continued, "It is because of what happened that we need your help. You see, we are going to try to change the Pattern of the Wheel."

As she spoke, the sun went down, and her face passed into the shadow. Behind her, the darkness began to thicken and take shape until it seemed to Jamie that he saw the figure of an old man standing there. Lucy gasped and he knew that she had seen it too, but Sara seemed unaware of the apparition behind her. The figure seemed not real, as she did, but insubstantial and grey. It reached out thin hands and placed them on her shoulders.

Lucy screamed. But Sara only raised one hand slowly and touched the thin fingers. "Are you there?" she asked softly.

At her touch the grey figure grew more substantial and Jamie saw that it was the old solicitor, the same old man who had come to see them on a rainy night in Camden Town: Mr Blunden of Blunden, Claverton and Smith. He moved slowly round to stand beside Sara. "Yes, I am here," he said.

Jamie could hardly recognize his voice, it seemed so full of sorrow. But Sara smiled at the old man and said, "Then you must help me to explain. You are so much cleverer than I am; will you tell them how it is possible to change the Pattern of the Wheel?"

When they were all settled on the seat by the sundial, with

Lucy feeling very sheepish at having been caught screaming for the second time, the old man began to explain.

"Sara has told you, I think, that time is not a straight line, endlessly passing, but more like a vast wheel, on the rim of which we stand at different points, except very rarely when we meet like this."

The children nodded to show that this, at least, was clear to them and he went on.

"I want you now to picture an infinite number of wheels, all turning in different directions, but all having the same still point at the centre."

He paused and Lucy thought hard. She felt that she had disgraced herself and she sought some way to regain their respect. So she struggled to grasp what he was saying and while Jamie was still scratching his head in perplexity, she said, "It would be like a round ball: all the wheels together would make up a great sphere ... like the earth itself."

The old man smiled and patted her hand and she did not flinch.

"A great sphere like the earth itself," he repeated, "but infinitely more vast. That great sphere is Time itself and Space and all Creation."

He paused and looked at them closely.

"I think I understand," said Lucy slowly, "but it's a bit difficult."

"Well, it's all Greek to me," said Jamie cheerfully, "but if you say that's how it is, I'll trust you!"

The old solicitor seemed strangely touched by this casual assertion. He said solemnly, "For that I am grateful. It is far more than I deserve." Then he fell silent.

Sara squeezed his hand. "Please go on," she said. "I can't stay very long: I only drank a very little."

"Forgive me," said the old man, "I was lost in thought." He turned again to Jamie and Lucy.

"You must understand," he told them, "that all the wheels are constantly crossing one another and that each one represents a different course of action. For at any given moment in time, a man has many different futures open to him, and yet all those possibilities have existed since time began. Your science books will tell you that nothing is ever really created or destroyed, and your Bible will tell you that there is nothing new under the sun. So that at any time, a man can choose which course he will take, but once he has chosen, he cannot turn back and undo what he has already done."

As he said this, he seemed quite overcome with gloom, and it was some time before he could continue.

"Once, long ago when I was alive, I made the wrong choice, not by chance, for that is easily forgiven, but through my own indifference, my own selfishness. I was guardian to Sara and George and I failed to guard them; I was their trustee but I was not worthy to be trusted. They came to me when they needed help, when no one else could help them, and I failed them. I would not listen to them, and as a result ... "

His voice broke and Sara said comfortingly, "It is all right, they know what happened; you need not say it."

The old man shook his head mournfully. "'It were better for such a man'," he said, "'that a mill-stone were hanged about his neck and he were drowned in the depths of the sea!'"

81

Sara sighed. "Oh, please don't take on so," she said. "It is all forgiven long ago."

Old Mr Blunden turned back to Jamie and Lucy who were watching him with helpless embarrassment.

"For a hundred years I have suffered," he told them. "I have been disgraced in my profession and tormented by my own conscience and to me it has been like a thousand years. But now, I have been given the chance to put right the terrible wrong I have done, and to bring my punishment to an end. To do this, I had first to obtain forgiveness, and Sara has forgiven me, though Georgie, I fear … "

"He is too young to understand," said Sara hastily. "You must not mind him."

"Ah, he is right to hate me," said the old man sorrowfully. But he went on, "Secondly, I must find someone who will trust me once again, someone who will trust me to guard him, even with his life. And lastly, I must go back to undo the harm I have caused and, with my own suffering, change the Pattern of the Wheel."

Jamie began to see what he had to do, and it no longer seemed like a game. "I am the one who has to trust you?" he said. "That's why you brought us here, why you came to Camden Town?"

The old man nodded.

"And it was you who wrote on the window, to tell Georgie and Sara about the book?"

"Yes, indeed. In the beginning it was not easy to make contact."

Jamie hesitated. He had an uneasy feeling that the old man was using them, as if he and the other children were all puppets and the old lawyer held the strings. And yet, if he was to be believed, he meant no harm, only to save Sara and Georgie from the dreadful fate he had once brought upon them. If he had just asked me to help him, he thought, it would have been easy, but do I really trust him ... ?

"It is not an easy thing, I know." The old man answered as if Jamie had spoken his thoughts aloud. "I have done nothing to deserve your trust. But alas, I did not make the conditions and there is no other way for the Pattern to be changed."

"What shall I have to do?" asked Jamie, trying to sound matter-of-fact.

"It is not yet clear," said the old man, "but whatever it may be, nothing shall harm you. I promise that I shall guard you from all dangers however they may come. I know I am not worthy, but I beg you to trust me for it is our only hope."

Jamie could not face the pleading eyes. He rose to his feet abruptly and went to lean on the sundial with his back to them all. He hated to make a promise unless he was certain that he could keep it. He tried to imagine what might lie ahead, and he knew in his heart that he was afraid.

He turned and said to Sara, "Have you forgiven him?"

She smiled and took the old man by the hand. "I have forgiven him," she said.

Impulsively, Jamie reached out his own hand. "Then I will trust him."

The old solicitor looked up at him as though he could not believe his good fortune. Then he reached out and grasped Jamie's hand in his own, which was cold and felt very fragile.

Jamie turned to Lucy who seemed rather left out. "You must trust him too," he said.

Lucy took his hand and said timidly, "I will try."

Sara took Lucy's other hand, and the circle was complete. "It is time to go," she said.

Now that the moment had come, Jamie and Lucy felt very nervous.

Lucy was clutching the little bottle which contained the brew of herbs. She uncorked it and looked at it anxiously. Suppose Sara had got the mixture wrong.

Jamie knew what she was thinking. He took the bottle from her and throwing back his head, gulped down half of it. It tasted bitter and he pulled a face but he seemed to feel the same as ever. He handed the bottle back to Lucy who raised it nervously to her lips. But though she was reluctant to drink it, she was even more unwilling to let Jamie go without her. As she began to drink, she comforted herself with the thought that no time would pass while they were away. She put down the bottle and stared at Jamie. She thought she saw something odd about his eyes, but it was hard to be sure. Her heart was beating very fast and she began to feel a strange stillness creeping through her limbs. She wanted to cry out, to call to Jamie, but her head began to spin faster and faster. She felt as if she were being sucked down into a vast whirlpool, deeper and deeper and deeper ...

Then everything became black.

Part Three

~~~~~~~~~~~~~~~~~~~~~~~~~~~~~~~~~~~~~~~

8

Lucy's head cleared and for a moment she thought that nothing had changed.

The sundial was still there and the garden seat, and Jamie was still holding her hand. He was looking at her rather anxiously so she smiled to reassure him that the dizziness had passed. She heard Sara saying cheerfully, "I felt like that the first time. I think it is more nervousness than anything, because I have never felt faint all the other times. Indeed, sometimes it is so easy, I hardly realize that I have changed."

Have I changed? thought Lucy wonderingly. Has anything changed? She noticed that the old solicitor had gone, but he could simply have walked away. She fancied that the plants growing around the sundial looked neater, that the trees in the distance did not loom so high, but in the twilight, it was hard to judge size and shape.

"Where are we?" she asked Jamie. She meant 'When are we?', for she could see very well where she was, but it seemed a silly question and she knew that Jamie would understand.

He said, "We are in Sara's time." He tried to say it calmly

so as not to alarm her, but it was impossible to keep the excitement out of his voice.

"It looks the same."

"Only from where you are standing," he said. "Now turn around slowly and don't be frightened by what you see."

Lucy gripped his hand as she turned around, but in spite of his warning her heart leaped into her mouth when she saw the great building that loomed up in the darkness with lights in the windows here and there.

"Where did it come from?" she gasped.

Jamie grinned. "You remember the old ruins?" he said. "Well, they couldn't have been as old as we thought. In Sara's time that building was still standing."

It was hard to see the details in the dim light, but by concentrating Lucy made out that the soaring arches, which she had taken for some old chapel, formed the front of a quite ugly Victorian-Gothic wing which had been added to the old house. Really, she thought, it looks better as a ruin. She was just wondering what could have happened to it, when she heard a low voice calling, "Sara, Miss Sara! Are you all right, miss?"

"Oh dear," said Sara. "Tom is growing anxious. He hates me to go into the garden alone at night, even for a moment, in case ... " She paused, not wanting to frighten Lucy. "We had better go and reassure him," she said.

She hurried off along the path with Jamie and Lucy following. As they drew near the house, they could see in the light from one of the windows the tall figure of a boy who came quickly towards them.

"Oh, there you are, miss," he began, "I was just ... "
Then he gasped and drew back in fear, staring at Jamie and
Lucy as they moved into the light. For a moment he hesitated,
then rushing forward he seized Sara and dragged her away
from them. He pushed her behind him and standing in
front of her, faced the children with the air of a man
confronting a savage bull.

"It's all right, miss!" he said. "They shan't harm you."

Sara stood on tiptoe and they saw her astonished eyes
peeping over the boy's shoulder. "Oh, Tom," she said,
"I didn't realize ... It is quite safe, I promise you. They are
friends of mine."

She came out from behind his back, and took Jamie and
Lucy by the hand. The boy seemed horrified and Lucy
wondered why he should be so put out. She glanced down
at herself to see if she looked the same as usual, and realized
with embarrassment that, compared with Sara's, her own
skirt was very short indeed. She had read that Victorians
were very prim and proper, but could the sight of her bare
knees be quite so terrible?

The boy swallowed hard. "Friends of yours, miss?" he
said incredulously. "Then I'm sure I'm very glad to see them.
You must have thought me very ill-mannered, miss, to seize
ahold of you like that. But with them being so strange and
misty like, I fancied I could see right through them and for
a moment, well ... " he hesitated, "I took them for ghosts,
miss!"

"We are all ghosts in a way," said Sara very gently. Jamie
saw that she was teasing and he laughed, but Lucy was too
busy peering at her fingers in the dim light, to see if anyone

87

could possibly see right through her. She did not like the thought at all.

"My friends are as real as you or I, Tom," went on Sara, "and they have come a very long way to help us."

"Then I welcome them, miss, for you are in need of friends," and, impulsively, the boy held out his hand.

Jamie realized what an effort it had cost him, having once taken Sara's hand in the same gesture of good faith. He grasped the hand and shook it warmly, and saw a look of wonder and relief grow on the boy's face.

"Why, Miss Sara," said Tom eagerly, "I seem to see them quite clearly now." He turned to Jamie. "It was all a trick of the light," he explained; "what a rare fool you must have thought me!"

"No," said Jamie, "I think you are very brave."

"So do I," said Sara, and the boy reddened awkwardly, seeing her smile at him.

As if to change the subject he said, "I see from the way you dress that you don't come from hereabouts. I suppose you wouldn't have come from the New World?" he added hopefully.

"Well, yes, I suppose you could say we have," said Jamie, feeling that the whole truth would be hard to explain.

The boy's face lit up. "They say 'tis a wonderful place, the New World!"

"Er ... yes, it is," agreed Jamie.

"Of course, 'tis a terrible long journey," Tom went on earnestly, "but 'tis one I plan to make myself one of these days. When I'm older, like, and Miss Sara has taught me to read and write, I mean to go there and try my fortune. They say there's a fine future in America for a young man as can read and write and ain't afraid of a bit of hard work!"

He seemed quite carried away in his enthusiasm, until Sara interrupted him, saying quietly, "How is my brother, Tom? Is he quite safe?"

Tom looked dismayed. "Oh, whatever must you think of me, Miss Sara, rambling on about myself? But he's safe enough, I promise you, though he must be growing hungry for he declares he will not touch their dry bread. He told me ... "

But they never learned what Georgie had told him for at that point, a harsh, demanding voice cut across the conversation.

"Sara!" it screamed. "Sara, where are you, you lazy slut!"

Sara turned pale and Tom clenched his fists angrily. "Oh, miss," he said, "if you'd only let me strike her down! I'm not a one to hit a woman, but she's a devil, miss, to say such things."

"Oh, Tom, please don't! Please go before she comes and finds you here. Go home to your supper; I know you must be hungry too. I will try to persuade her to let Georgie out. She cannot remain angry for ever."

As the boy hesitated, the voice came again, only closer now.

"Sara! You wait till I find yer, you little hussy. 'Anging around in the bushes with that garden boy, I don't doubt. I know what you're up to, miss!"

Tom flamed with anger. "Oh, let me stay and face her," he begged. "I'm not afraid of her. You know I'd die for you, Miss Sara!"

"I know, Tom," said Sara, "but she will only dismiss you and I shall lose the last friend I have. Now, go quickly, for my sake!"

Tom groaned with despair. "Well, I shan't go far, miss," he said. "If you need me, you have only to call from the nursery window." Then he turned and vanished into the darkness.

"Should we go with him?" asked Lucy nervously. "We don't want her to know that we are here." The truth was that she was afraid to face the woman whose heavy footsteps could be heard lurching towards them along the path.

But to her surprise, Sara said, "No, keep still where you are. I think it will be all right."

Lucy moved a little closer to Jamie, and they stood in the shadows behind Sara as a huge woman with a mean, ugly face and a wide flat nose came shuffling into the light of the window.

"So there you are," she hissed when she saw Sara, "and all alone, I see. But 'oo was 'ere with you a moment ago? One of them vulgar servants, I'll be bound. Not only 'ave you got no sense, miss; you ain't got no taste, neither. I don't know 'ow a gent like your dear uncle can abide 'avin' you in the same 'ouse. An' settin' such a bad example to my dear Bella an' all!"

"I'm very sorry," said Sara meekly, "but I only came out to speak a word to poor Georgie, through the grating there. Oh, Mrs Wickens, won't you please let him out? He's only a child and it is so dark in there!"

Jamie was furious. It made him sick to hear Sara speak so humbly to a coarse old woman who was not fit to polish her shoes. How can she do it? he thought; I'd rather die.

But Lucy understood. She knew that it took more courage for Sara to humble herself than for her to defy the old woman, and she saw that, for Georgie's sake, the older girl would sacrifice herself in any way.

"Don't talk to me about that brat!" roared the old woman. "After the things 'ee said to me, 'ee'll be lucky if 'ee gets out before next week."

"Oh, but please ... "

"None of your cheek, miss!" and Mrs Wickens swung her fat fist at Sara.

It was more than Jamie could stand. He ran forward out of the shadows and pushed the old woman away. "Leave her alone!" he shouted. "You rotten old bully!"

Lucy was horrified. Now, she thought, Jamie would be locked in the cellar too.

But to her surprise, Mrs Wickens did not seem to see him. She felt the force as he pushed her, and she staggered drunkenly. "What's that?" she muttered. " 'oo did that? That murdering gardener's boy, I'll be bound."

Jamie faced her. "No, it wasn't," he said, "it was me, and what's more I'll do it again if you touch Sara."

The old woman looked straight through him as though he were not there.

We are ghosts, thought Lucy as the truth struck her for the first time; Jamie and I are ghosts!

Mrs Wickens was still muttering angrily, " 'Ee'll have to go. I've seen 'im snoopin' around in the bushes ... "

"I tell you it was me!" shouted Jamie angrily.

Lucy walked forward out of the shadows and touched his arm.

"You keep back, Lucy," he said. "I'll deal with her."

"She can't see you," said Lucy quietly. "She doesn't even know you are there."

Jamie faltered in his anger and looked uncertainly from Lucy to the old woman and back again. Now that he paused to consider, he realized that there was something very odd about the way the woman ignored him. He waved one hand in front of her bloodshot eyes but there was not the slightest flicker of reaction.

"I do believe you're right," he said. "She doesn't seem to hear me either. Do you think she's had some kind of fit?"

"There's nothing wrong with her," said Lucy, "it's us. We are ghosts!" Now that she was growing used to the idea, she rather enjoyed the sight of Jamie's astonishment.

"But we can't ... " he began, then stopped, peered at his hand, and found it solid. "We can't be!" he said incredulously.

"Ask Sara," said Lucy.

Jamie turned to Sara. "Are we?" he said.

Sara hesitated, glanced at the old woman who was beating around in the bushes for the elusive gardener's boy and, finding her busy, nodded violently.

"But Tom could see us; why can't she?" he demanded.

Sara glanced nervously at Mrs Wickens. "Too old," she hissed, "too insensitive."

"Remember what Sara told us?" said Lucy eagerly. "When she and Georgie came to our time, they found

92

that most people could not see them. She said that only children, or people who were very ... "

But she was interrupted by the old woman who had caught Sara's whispered words. "Old!" she screamed. "Insensitive!"

"No, no," said Sara quickly, "I said my hands were growing cold and insensitive. It is the night wind."

It wasn't a very good lie, but Mrs Wickens was prepared to accept it rather than be called 'old'.

"And 'oo's fault is that, miss?" she sneered. "If you will sneak out to keep your assignations ... Get inside now. Up to the schoolroom and be quick about it!"

"But Georgie ... ?" Sara tried once more.

"He stays where he is. Now be off with you."

Sara's head drooped miserably as she made her way into the house, followed by the old woman.

Lucy glanced at Jamie. He shrugged his shoulders and then nodded, and they went after the others up the steps and through the front door.

It was strange to walk into the same house and to find it so different. Not only were the pale dust-sheets gone but also the simple pieces of old furniture beneath them. Gone were the old Persian carpets with their lovely faded patterns and the delicately coloured curtains. In their place there was massive ugly furniture in ox-blood mahogany, heavy folds of dusty plush and a terrible abundance of hideous ornaments. The walls were sombrely papered, the floors darkly carpeted, and the air smelt indescribably stale.

Jamie wrinkled his nose. "Place wants a good clean," he said loudly, as they made their way upstairs. His voice, echoing and re-echoing around the high roof, reminded

Lucy of the long-dead voices which had whispered in the empty house, like old family keepsakes in a great box.

Mrs Wickens had obviously set out to escort Sara to the schoolroom, but she was too fat for the stairs and she was already puffing. She called out and a thin-faced maid appeared from nowhere.

"Meakin," she said, "take Miss Sara up to the schoolroom and lock her in." Then she collapsed panting on to an overstuffed sofa.

The maid, who seemed to have a thin line for a mouth, bobbed ingratiatingly. "Yes, ma'am," she said.

But as they turned to go, a high, childlike voice called, "Mama, Mama! see my new pink silk!" and along the passage-way came a girl of about seventeen. She was plump but pretty, with fair hair in a mass of ringlets and china-blue eyes. Her round cheeks too were like china, white with a faint touch of pink, and, like a china doll's, her expression was quite blank.

Mrs Wickens lolled back on the sofa fanning herself with one hand. A look of smug satisfaction spread over her face.

"Bella, me love, you are a picture," she said, in a voice of oily sweetness. "Turn around and let Mama see yer."

Bella held out the skirt of the pink dress and revolved vacantly like a dancing doll on a music-box.

"Lovely, my pet, lovely. Bertie will be struck all of a 'eap when 'ee sees yer."

Arabella smiled like a well-fed cat and turned to Sara. " 'Ain't it pretty, Sal?" she said.

"Very pretty," said Sara who, to Lucy's surprise, seemed quite to like this stupid-looking, doll-like girl. Lucy was not unkind but it irked her to see Sara in her threadbare dress, admiring this plump creature in her ridiculous flounces.

Safe in the knowledge that only Sara and Jamie could hear her, she remarked loudly and clearly, "*I* think she looks like a stuffed, pink pig!"

The effect was startling.

Bella's jaw dropped and she swung round to stare at Lucy. Then she opened her rose-bud mouth and screamed and screamed.

Confusion reigned. Meakin, the maid, and old Mrs Wickens ran to calm her.

"What is it?" Lucy turned nervously to Sara. "Surely she can't see me."

Sara frowned. "I think perhaps she can," she said softly. "I should have realized. She looks very grown-up, but she has the mind of a child. She can probably just see you in a thin, transparent way."

Bella's screaming died to a whimper. She pointed at Lucy with a shaking hand. "What is it?" she said. "It's a ghost, I swear it is! I can see right through it!"

Mrs Wickens stared at Lucy. " 'Ush now," she said, "there ain't nothing there, you silly gel. 'Ere, let's smell yer breath. You ain't been at me gin again, 'ave yer? I told yer before, Bertie don't like it!"

"But I 'aven't, Ma, I 'aven't!" said Bella desperately.

Then Lucy had a brilliant idea. It would be cruel to tease the simple Bella, she thought, and yet it was crueller still to shut a little boy in a pitch-dark cellar. Perhaps Bella would have some influence on her mother.

Slowly she raised one arm and pointed at the quaking girl.

95

"Hear me, Bella," she said, trying to sound as imposing as possible, "I shall haunt you until little Georgie is released from the cellar."

Sara flashed her a look of gratitude, and Jamie murmured, "Oh, very cunning! Well done, Lucy."

Bella clutched at her mother. "Let Georgie out of the cellar, Ma," she pleaded, "then maybe it'll go away."

"What'll go away?" The old woman looked impatient. "I already told yer, there ain't nothin' there."

"But there is, Ma, there is!"

Jamie felt perhaps he should increase the pressure. Besides, it looked like fun to act the ghost, and he wished he had thought of it first.

"Let Georgie g-o-o-o-o," he moaned in a sepulchral voice, waving his arms in the air as he imagined a bona fide ghost would do.

But the appearance of a second, and even more frightening vision, was more than poor Bella could stand. With a piercing scream, she fainted clean away, falling to the floor like a crumpled rose.

Sara, Meakin, and old Mrs Wickens clustered anxiously around her.

Lucy glared at the crestfallen Jamie. "Trust you to overdo it," she said sourly.

There was a sound of footsteps hurrying along the corridor and a young man appeared. He was tall and thin, with dark hair parted in the centre and neat side-whiskers. He had a smooth round face with slightly protruding eyes.

"What is this?" he cried in a high-pitched, anxious voice. "I heard someone screaming."

96

Meakin stepped aside to reveal the pink heap of Bella lying on the floor. The young man turned pale.

"Bella, my love!" He knelt down beside her and clutched her hand.

Bella opened her round, blue eyes and gazed about her blankly. Then seeing the young man, she threw her arms round his neck.

"Oh, Bertie," she said, "I was that scared! Tell Ma to let 'im out, Bertie, or they'll be after me again." And she began to wail at the very thought of it.

"Let who out? Who is after you, Bella dearest? What is all this about, Mrs Wickens?"

He turned on the old woman angrily, and at once she became flustered and apologetic as she tried to explain how Georgie came to be in the cellar.

"Go and release the child immediately," snapped Bertie. "I won't have Bella distressed. And Meakin, fetch the smelling salts from Miss Bella's room."

The maid hurried off along the passage, but Mrs Wickens remained.

"Well," said Bertie crossly, "why are you waiting?"

The old woman simpered. "Oh, Bertie, 'ow can I leave me precious child while she's like this."

"Bella is perfectly all right with me," said Bertie coldly. "Now go and do as I say."

"But Bertie, all them stairs ... Me 'eart won't stand it."

"I'll go," said Sara quickly.

Mrs Wickens grumbled but she parted with the key which hung from a chatelaine at her belt, and by the time Meakin had returned with the smelling salts, Sara's swift feet had taken her down to the cellar and back with a rather coal-dusty, angry Georgie.

"Take them to the schoolroom, Meakin, and lock them both in," ordered the old woman. She lowered her voice to a hiss so that Bertie would not hear. "I shall deal with them two later," she said, and her mouth set into a grim hard line.

9

"IF ONLY we knew just what they are planning to do," said Lucy, "it would make things a lot easier."

"Yes, and what time they are planning to do it," added Jamie.

The four children were sitting together in the schoolroom at the top of the house. It was a large, bleak room and at first Lucy could not place it, although she had explored the old house thoroughly and thought she knew every room. Then she realized that this was the top floor of the ugly Victorian wing which had been destroyed in the fire and which remained, in their own time, only as a creeper-covered ruin. The thought made her uneasy.

The room contained only a few battered oddments of furniture which had been thrown out of other parts of the house. The floor had a small, badly worn rug in front of the fireplace but otherwise the boards were bare. It was cold, too, for the thin warmth of the spring sunlight had gone and there was no fire to break the gathering chill of the night.

Jamie and Lucy had found no difficulty in getting into the schoolroom since Meakin, in the general confusion, had left the key in the lock of the door.

Jamie had been disappointed to find that he could not pass

through walls. "I can't understand it," he said. "In all the ghost stories I've ever read, the ghosts can go back and forwards through solid oak doors without any trouble. I mean, it's one way of telling that they are ghosts."

"We had the same trouble," agreed Sara sympathetically. "When we first arrived in your time, Georgie got a nasty bruise trying to pass through a garden wall to save going round by the gate. It is my belief that it only happens when the 'ghost' you see is someone still in his own time who passes through something built at a later period."

Jamie considered the idea. "I expect you're right," he said, his voice tinged with admiration. Sara was clever, he thought, like Lucy but without Lucy's timid ways. He wished that they did not belong to different times. Most of the girls he had met were so silly and giggled all the time; but Sara was almost as good as a boy, better in some ways.

Not being able to pass through doors meant that Jamie and Lucy dared not risk being locked in with the Victorian children. So they had unlocked the door and hidden the key under the stair-carpet.

"Meakin will get the blame for losing it," said Georgie gleefully, "and it will serve her right, for she's a rotten spy." And he went around shouting "Sneakin' Meakin" with obvious delight.

Lucy thought he was a rather spiteful child, but she remembered that he had grown up with no parents and tried to make allowances. She saw that Sara, who knew him best, loved him dearly, so she told herself he must be good at heart. But sometimes she suspected that Sara, having no other family, was simply blind to his faults.

"It's like sitting on a time-bomb and waiting for it to go off," complained Jamie, and then had to explain to Georgie what a time-bomb was. The little boy was delighted with this invention, and ran about the schoolroom shouting, "A time-bomb under Mrs Wickens... BOOM! A time-bomb under Uncle Bertie ... BOOM!"

"He makes a great deal of noise," said Sara smiling, "but it is easier to talk about what might happen, if he cannot hear us. He is so young, he should not have to think of death."

He seems to enjoy thinking about everyone else's, thought Lucy, but she knew she was being unkind, and that all little boys pretended to kill people.

"Perhaps Lucy and I should go and eavesdrop," said Jamie, "and see if we can find what they are up to."

"You will learn nothing now, however hard you listen," Sara told him. "They are all gone in to dinner and they will not dare to speak of such things while Mr Blunden is there. He is a foolish man but I am sure he is not bad. Besides, he thinks too highly of his profession to be a party to any unlawful plots."

"Do you mean old Mr Blunden, the solicitor?" Lucy was surprised. "What is he doing here in the house?"

"He has come to see Uncle Bertie on business. I think our uncle needs more money, and he is trying to persuade Mr Blunden to arrange a loan for him."

"But surely he will help you," said Lucy. "We must tell him everything and persuade him to take you away from here."

Sara sighed. "You know we have already written to him," she said. "I fear he does not believe us."

"But he would if you talked to him," said Jamie. "After all, your letter could have gone astray." Sara seemed doubtful and he went on earnestly, "Don't forget that he brought us here from Camden Town. If it wasn't for him, we shouldn't be here at all."

"Yes," said Lucy, "and the sexton told us that Mr Blunden was terribly upset when he came back after the fire and found ... " she left the sentence unfinished.

Sara shook her head. "It's not the same man," she said. "At least, it is the same, and yet it is not." She frowned. "It's very hard to explain, but the Mr Blunden who is downstairs now, just does not know how sorry he is going to be."

"Then you must tell him," said Jamie firmly. "We must make him understand or at least we must try. You have nothing to lose now that time is so short. They can only lock you up again and then you will be no worse off than before."

Sara thought of the beatings she had had from Mrs Wickens in the past, and she was about to argue the point. But it came to her clearly that a beating was nothing compared to the fire.

"Very well," she said calmly. "We will go down and hide in the bushes opposite the front door, and try to catch him as he leaves. Out there we shall have more chance of speaking to him before they can stop us."

"Shall we leave Georgie up here?" asked Lucy hopefully. "It's very damp out there."

"Oh, no," said Sara anxiously, "I cannot feel safe unless he is near us."

"Then he'd better leave his time-bombs behind," said Jamie, putting his hands over his ears as a particularly loud one went off under his chair. He turned to Georgie sternly. "Listen," he said, "we are going downstairs to hide and you'll have to be very quiet, do you hear?"

The little boy stuck out his chin. "You are just a silly old ghost," he said, "and you can't tell me what to do!"

"Georgie," said his sister quickly, "we are going to play hunters in the African jungle. The one who is quietest will be the chief."

Georgie froze into a mouselike stillness.

I just don't have the knack, thought Jamie.

It seemed to Lucy that they had been sitting on the rain-wet seat in the cold, damp shrubbery for hours. Georgie had been miserable and aggravating by turns and at last, to everyone's relief, he had fallen asleep wrapped about in Sara's old cloak and with his head on her shoulder.

I'm uncomfortable enough myself, thought Lucy, wriggling into a new position, but she must be cramped all over sitting still like that so as not to waken him. And yet she doesn't complain. She stared at Sara. Her eyes were closed and her pretty face looked thin and tired. Lucy thought how often she herself had wallowed in self-pity since her father had died, wondering again and again why it should have happened to her. Yet Sara had lost father and mother; she had no older brother to lean upon, only a temperamental child to whom she must be everything. And in spite of all this, she had not once complained.

Lucy drifted into a day dream in which she herself was

strong and brave, beautiful and uncomplaining, and in which boys like Tom and Jamie fell over each other to be of service to her. But her dream was rudely shattered by the sound of horses' hooves and by Jamie shaking her.

"Wake up, Lucy, they'll be coming out at any moment."

"I wasn't asleep," she said guiltily, and opening her eyes she saw that a carriage had drawn up at the door of the house. Sara was sitting upright now and staring nervously towards it.

"Shall I take Georgie," Lucy offered, "if you don't want to wake him?"

"I hate to disturb him," Sara admitted, "but I think the sight of him is more likely to soften the old man's heart."

Georgie woke irritably, rubbing his eyes and beginning to grizzle. Jamie and Lucy both thought that Sara herself was far more likely to soften anyone's heart, but they did not like to say so.

"I know you are tired, Georgie dear," she was saying, "but we must ask Mr Blunden to help us, so do be patient."

Georgie stuck out his lower lip. "Blunden is an old fool," he said, "and I hate him."

The door of the house swung open and the old solicitor appeared on the porch. But to their surprise, they saw that the children's uncle was beside him, dressed in travelling clothes. Bella clung to his arm and she was pouting miserably. Her high-pitched voice carried across to the shrubbery.

"Dearest Bertie, do you 'ave to go? Poor Bella will be so sad without you."

"Oh, if he is going too, then we are really lost," breathed

Sara. "It was some comfort to have him in the house, for though he is foolish, he is not really wicked."

Bertie was consoling the clinging Bella. "It will be only a night or two, my pet, but Mr Blunden thinks it advisable that I go with him to London. Now don't cry for it must be so, and you will only spoil your pretty eyes. There will be papers to sign and it will save a great deal of time, and I must get some money soon or, dash it, there will be no more silk dresses for you."

The old solicitor came down the steps towards the carriage. Sara took a deep breath.

"Now, Georgie," she said, "or we shall be too late," and she ran across the gravelled courtyard pulling him by the hand.

Lucy and Jamie watched anxiously as she approached the old man and began to speak to him.

The wind was growing stronger and her soft voice was blown away, but it was plain from her earnest face and pleading hands what she was saying.

"Oh, surely he will listen to her," said Lucy. "He is a kind man, I know he is."

The old man seemed startled by the sudden appearance of his wards out of the dark night. He bent to hear what Sara was saying but as he listened his face grew embarrassed and then annoyed. He wagged a finger at the children and Jamie and Lucy caught the words "mischievous children ... " and "a kind and considerate guardian".

Sara raised her voice. "But it is Mrs Wickens, she means to harm us, I know. Oh, you must not leave us here alone with her."

Mr Blunden looked shocked and for a moment Lucy thought he was convinced. But then he frowned and turned to the children's uncle who, in his efforts to escape the clinging Bella, had not noticed their arrival. As the old man spoke to him, Bertie's face fell and his eyes seemed to protrude more than ever. Bella looked most indignant and they heard her cry, "She cannot mean to accuse Mama!"

Bertie patted her plump arm. "Of course not, dearest," he soothed. "We all know that your mother is a splendid woman."

This was more than Georgie could stand. They heard him shout, "Her mother is a drunken old witch!" just as Mrs Wickens herself came sweeping out of the door to see what the noise was all about.

She nearly exploded. " 'Ow did them kids get out?" she shrieked. "You wait till I see that there Meakin ... Lyin' little troublemakers, you are, the pair of you. You shall both go in the cellar, and I'll see to it myself ... "

Her voice was lost in the general confusion that followed. Georgie was shouting insults, Bella was bawling like a lost calf, Bertie was pleading with her, Mr Blunden was scolding the children, and through it all, Sara stood quietly weeping.

"Oh, I can't bear it," said Lucy. "How can they treat her so? She is so gentle. And that stupid old man: I thought he was so nice."

"I shall go and speak to them myself," said Jamie. "Perhaps if he sees me, he will remember what is going to happen."

"But it hasn't happened yet," said Lucy, "so how can he remember it?"

"Well, he must remember something. After all, he brought us here."

But as he moved forward, he felt a hand upon his shoulder and turning he jumped at the sight of the old solicitor standing behind him. He stared incredulously for a moment then looked back at the figure of Mr Blunden on the steps.

"But ... there are two of you!" he said.

Lucy turned in surprise, hearing him speak, and though the apparition startled her at first, she found it strangely comforting.

"Yes, there are two of us," said the old man sadly, "though we are the same man. We are separated by a great gulf of time and knowledge. But he would not know you; it was I who brought you here."

Jamie was growing hopelessly confused. "But surely if I told him ... " he began.

The old man shook his head. "He would not hear you, he would not even see you. He is a shallow, insensitive man, incapable of visions. If it were not so, I would plead with him myself."

Jamie saw that there were tears running down his cheeks, and looking from one man to the other, so much alike and yet so different, he decided that it was all too much for him to understand. Lucy, who usually screamed and ran, seemed to accept this weird situation without difficulty; she seemed almost glad to have the wraithlike figure beside her. Jamie sighed in perplexity. There was only one thing he did understand, and that was that he was unlikely to be seen whatever he did. He turned and moved quietly away through the bushes.

Lucy stood beside the old man and watched the distressing scene on the porch.

"It's all so difficult," she sighed. "We have come here to help, but there seems to be so little we can do."

"It is not yet time," said the old man sadly. "For the time being, everything will go on as before. You see, the others cannot change the past: they must fulfil the pattern they have already created. Only you and your brother, coming from another time, can change the Pattern of the Wheel. But not yet. Now you can only wait, and for a while be patient. When the time for action has come, I will return, never fear ... " His voice seemed to be fading. "Tell your brother I shall come ... "

The words were lost on the passing wind and turning to catch them, Lucy found that he had gone. She turned back towards the porch. Bertie and the old solicitor were in the carriage and the driver was gathering up the reins. Sara and Georgie were walking forlornly up the steps into the house with Mrs Wickens storming after them.

In a flurry of hooves and turning wheels, the carriage moved off along the drive. Bella waved until it was out of sight; then she too went back into the house. The door slammed shut and all was quiet.

Lucy turned to speak to Jamie but he was not there. She looked about her anxiously; he was nowhere to be seen. She called to him: there was no answer. Her heart began to hurry as she realized that she was alone.

She had always been afraid to be out in the dark by herself, even if it was only to go as far as the coalshed. But she had learned to keep her fear under control and not to give way to the shudders until she was safely back in the kitchen with the door closed. Now she found herself alone with no door against darkness, no safe, warm place to run to. It came to her suddenly that if she never found Jamie again, she would be utterly lost in time as well as space.

Panic seized her, and she began to run blindly through the dark bushes, calling his name over and over again. Her heart was pounding and she seemed unable to catch her breath. She paused gasping and in the windy quietness she heard footsteps coming along a path near by. She plunged towards the sound and saw a dark figure moving through the night.

"Oh, Jamie," she sobbed, "thank goodness I've found you ... " But as she almost collided with the looming figure, she saw that it was much too tall to be Jamie. Out of the shadow of the bushes came a huge, shambling man with a great bundle of wood in his arms. His lurching shape was so close that she could hear his animal-like breathing. Lucy screamed and ran desperately away through the high, wet bushes.

The moon had come out and threw a nightmare jigsaw of light and shadow over everything so that she could not see the ground and stumbled as she ran. To her horror, she heard the big man give a hoarse cry and come blundering after her.

Then, just when it seemed to Lucy that it was all a terrible dream and that she must either wake or die, she felt her arm seized roughly and she was pulled to one side. A hand went over her mouth and a voice said, "For heaven's sake, Lucy, it's only me!" She stumbled and fell to the ground, crying with relief.

"Keep very still," said Jamie. "He can't see you, remember, and he can't hear your voice, but he can hear the bushes rustling as you move among them. Keep absolutely still, and he will go away."

Now that she had found him again, Lucy would have obeyed if Jamie had told her to stand on her head, anything so long as she did not have to be alone in the hostile darkness.

"But who is it?" she hissed. "He was more like a monster than a man."

"I think it's Mr Wickens, the old prizefighter," whispered Jamie. "Sara said he was a mindless mountain."

As they crouched motionless beneath the bush, Lucy became aware of a sweet, powerful perfume like a waterfall around them. It seemed mysteriously familiar and glancing upwards she saw great pale blossoms gleaming in the moonlight. It was an early rhododendron in full flower. Surely, she thought, they can't be the same flowers that I was picking for the house only ... was it yesterday? She realized with a start that her yesterday was a hundred years away and she wondered whether a rhododendron could live that long.

Stumbling footsteps and a rough voice called, "'Oo's there then ... ? I can see yer!"

Jamie gripped Lucy's hand and they held their breath.

The big man snorted. "Cats!" he said scornfully, "or them blamed foxes." And he shuffled away into the darkness.

When it seemed safe to talk again, Jamie said crossly, "Whatever were you playing at: tearing around in the bushes, screaming your head off! It's a good thing that ugly great ox couldn't hear you."

Lucy felt rather put out that he, not being so short of breath, had got his reproaches in first, when it was clearly she who had been wronged.

"You just disappeared," she said indignantly. "Why did you run off and leave me alone in the dark?"

"I left you with old Blunden."

"Thanks a lot," said Lucy bitterly; "only he promptly dissolved into thin air which wasn't very reassuring."

Jamie saw that she had a good case, so he changed his tactics.

"Well, anyway," he said, "I was doing something useful. You remember the old sexton said that Mr Blunden came back when he saw the fire, but he was too late?"

Lucy nodded.

"Well, I've made certain that they'll be back a lot sooner. I've cut the harness on the horses half through with my penknife. They won't get far before it snaps."

Lucy sighed, "I don't think it will make any difference," she said. "It's not time yet," and she told him what the old lawyer had said.

"But if the traces break ... " protested Jamie.

"Perhaps it would have happened anyway: the old sexton said the carriage broke down."

Jamie remembered that she was right and he felt very deflated. He had been rather proud of his exploit.

"Well, I think old Blunden is wrong," he said crossly, "but I'm not going to argue about it. We had better sneak back into the house and see what has happened to Sara and Georgie. We'll only get pneumonia if we sit out here."

10

HALF-AN-HOUR later, Lucy and Jamie were sitting on the stairs not far from the schoolroom door. It was warmer and drier than in the shrubbery outside, but their mood was, if anything, even gloomier.

It had taken them a little while to find Georgie and Sara. Jamie had expected to find them banished to the cellar again, and they had wasted some time blundering through the coal cellars and wine cellars in the dark, getting dirty and cross but finding no one.

And all the time the two Victorian children had been locked in the comparative safety of the night nursery next to the schoolroom. This time Mrs Wickens herself had been their jailor and she had chosen the nursery when she found the schoolroom key was missing.

Sara assured them through the keyhole that they were really quite happy. They were sitting on the bed, they had a stump of candle, and she was reading Georgie a story.

Lucy and Jamie had retired to the stairs to think things out.

"Of course, Sara is only putting on an act to stop Georgie being frightened," said Lucy. "She must be terrified really."

"Sara's not the sort of girl who terrifies easily," said Jamie admiringly.

Lucy, still smarting from the memory of her panic in the

garden, took this as a personal reproach. She sniffed miserably. "I should never have come," she said. "I can't help it if I get frightened in the dark."

It took Jamie a moment or two to get to the bottom of this remark. When he did he said, "Oh, don't be a ninny. I wasn't getting at you. After all, no one would expect you to be as brave as Sara; you've always had me around to look after you."

He said it with a certain smugness but Lucy decided to let it pass.

"Why do you suppose Mrs Wickens changed her mind?" she asked. "Locking them up here, I mean, instead of in the cellar?"

"Maybe Bella put in a word for them," said Jamie. "She's really not too bad ... Bella, not her mother. I wonder how that old hag came to have such a pretty daughter."

Lucy was not prepared to discuss Bella's charms; she thought her much too fat.

"It's right over the library," she said.

Jamie stopped thinking about Bella's blue eyes and considered the library. Lucy's remarks were so cryptic. Suddenly he saw what she was getting at. "Oh, Lord," he groaned, "of course, that's where the fire started. They'd have been safer in the cellar."

"It's all happening just as it did before," said Lucy. "Mr Blunden said it would."

"Then what's the use of being here at all?" said Jamie angrily. "The people we want to talk to can't see us or hear us, and if they can, like Bella, they promptly have hysterics."

"It was the same for Sara when she came to our time,"

agreed Lucy. "It's really very frustrating being a ghost. No wonder poor Mr Blunden was reduced to writing on steamy windows."

"When we *do* do something," continued Jamie, who wasn't listening to her, "we find we still haven't changed anything. We just seem to fit into some pattern which was always there."

"The Pattern of the Wheel," said Lucy thoughtfully. "But it can be changed, Jamie, or why would he bring us here? It's only that the time hasn't come yet. Mr Blunden said that when ... "

"Mr Blunden, Mr Blunden!" said Jamie irritably. "Do you really think we can trust what he says?"

Lucy stared at him in dismay. "Jamie, you *must* trust him," she said. "If you don't, nothing *can* be changed. You remember what he said: he could only change the pattern if Sara would forgive him and you would trust him."

"There you go again," said Jamie. "It's always 'He said this' and 'He said that'." He was silent for a moment: then he growled, "Look at the way he spoke to Sara; he actually made her cry and she's not the sort who cries easily."

Lucy was too alarmed to care if this was a slight or not.

"Jamie, you must trust him!" she begged. "You promised to trust him in spite of the bad things he had done. That was one of the conditions."

"Maybe it was" — Jamie's jaw set stubbornly — "but that was before I had seen him doing it. I don't think I could trust him now."

"Oh, Jamie!" Lucy saw from his face that it was useless to argue with him and she began to be afraid. A terrible sense of disaster seemed to eat at the edges of her mind. She knew, though she could not begin to explain it, that what was required of Jamie was an act of faith: he must give his trust to a man he knew to be unworthy of it, or there could not be a second chance. And if there was not ...

"For Sara's sake," she said desperately. "You must trust him for Sara's sake." Surely, she thought, this appeal would reach him.

"I can save her by myself," said Jamie obstinately.

"But that's just what you can't do. You can't change the pattern single-handed. Mr Blunden said ..."

"Mr Blunden said ... " Jamie did a very mean imitation of her voice, high-pitched with nervousness. "I'm sick of hearing his name, Lucy. I tell you I can save them by myself. We know more or less what is going to happen and forewarned is forearmed. I shall get hold of the keys and when the fire starts I shall just unlock the door and let Sara and Georgie out."

Lucy was too miserable to answer. She knew in her heart that it could not be that easy, and if anything happened to Jamie ... Perhaps he would never get back; perhaps he would be altogether lost in Time. The silence lengthened as she struggled to find the words with which to convince him.

There were footsteps on the landing below.

"Quick!" said Jamie. "We'd better get out of sight."

"They can't see us," said Lucy dully.

"Bella can, and it sounds like her step: light and a bit bouncy."

They drew back into the shadows of the upper landing

and it was indeed Bella. She came up the stairs to the nursery carrying a tray with two mugs of steaming milk and a plate of biscuits. She unlocked the door and went inside.

"Get the key," hissed Lucy.

"It's no use," said Jamie. "If we take it now, so that she can't lock them in, she will tell her mother and the old battleaxe will move them to another room. We have to take the key without anyone noticing. When she comes out, we must follow her and see what she does with it."

Five minutes later, Bella emerged with the empty mugs. She locked the door, put the key on the tray and went downstairs.

Jamie and Lucy tiptoed after her and reached the landing just in time to see her vanishing down the long corridor. As she arrived at the top of the main staircase, her mother joined her.

"Well, did they drink it all?" she demanded.

Bella nodded. "They were real 'ungry," she said, "but Sara wouldn't eat the biscuits; she made Georgie 'ave them all."

"Then let 'er go 'ungry, little fool," said Mrs Wickens crossly, "if that's all the thanks I get for me kindness."

"It was more than they deserved after saying them awful things. I should 'ope they'd be very grateful to you."

Mrs Wickens seized her arm. "But you didn't say as I sent it?"

Bella squealed. "Oh, Ma, you're 'urtin' me arm. I said as you told me, that I was doin' it secretly out of the kindness of me 'eart."

A slow smile spread over the old woman's face. "That's a

good girl," she said, "only I don't want 'em to think I'm gettin' soft, see. Now be a good child and take that tray back to the kitchen."

She took the key from the tray and, while Bella went on downstairs, fastened it to the great chatelaine of keys that hung from her belt. Then she smiled to herself. "Me gettin' soft!" she repeated as if she found it amusing and she began to laugh.

"Quickly, now," said Jamie who had been waiting his chance. "We must get that key from her."

"What do you think she meant ... " began Lucy, but he was already away down the passage in pursuit of Mrs Wickens.

Lucy sighed and went after him.

It was a strange feeling to walk so close to the old woman knowing that she could neither see nor hear them.

Jamie turned to Lucy. "Run ahead of her," he said, "and do something to make her stop."

"But she can't see me."

"Well knock something over, smash an ornament, anything so long as she stands still for a moment. If I try to undo the key while she's moving, she may feel it pulling."

Lucy ran ahead of the old woman, almost brushing against her as she passed. She glanced back and it was rather unnerving to see that she really was invisible. It made her feel somehow less than human.

There was a vase on a side-table and she reached towards it. But it was an old vase of a lovely shade of blue and it looked strangely familiar. She realized suddenly that she had seen it before, that it stood in the drawing-room of the house in her own time. Does that mean that I can't break it, she thought, since it is still there a hundred years from now? Or if I do break it, will it be gone when I get back? Her hands were round it, but she hesitated.

"Oh, stop dithering!" Jamie's exasperated voice jerked her into action. She let go of the vase, then grabbing at a gilt-framed painting on the wall, swung it sideways so that it hung at a grotesque angle.

Mrs Wickens stopped dead and stared at the painting. "Oh, my Gawd!" she exclaimed, "that give me a fright! Whatever made it move like that? Must be the wind, I s'pose." She looked about her nervously, then reached up to straighten it.

Jamie took hold of the thin belt that held the chatelaine and cut through it with his pen-knife. But the heavy key-ring slipped from his grasp and fell to the floor with a crash.

The old woman swore and letting go of the painting, grabbed at her belt. "Now me belt's broke," she muttered crossly and she bent to pick up the key-ring just as James told hold of it. She saw it move in his hand and gave a frightened shriek. "'Elp, this place is 'aunted!" She made a sudden grab at the keys, taking Jamie by surprise, and tore them out of his hand. Then gathering up her skirts, she ran down the passage and into her room, slamming the door behind her.

Her ungainly figure with the fat legs and her awkward gait, made her look like a pantomime dame. Jamie thought that it would have been very funny if it had not been so serious. He ran to the door and tried to open it, but even as he turned the handle he heard her shriek again and the key grated in the lock.

Jamie stood and fumed at his own clumsiness.

Lucy tried to comfort him. "It wasn't your fault," she said. "It just isn't time yet, so it's no use trying to change things."

Jamie did not trust himself to answer. He snorted and stalked away towards the stairs.

"Where are you going?"

"I'm going to climb in through her window. We have to get those keys somehow."

Lucy sighed. It was no use arguing with him. She wandered slowly after him. When she reached the blue vase, she stopped and touched it gently. I couldn't break it, she thought, because it still exists in our own time, just as the grave exists in the churchyard. She picked up the vase with a sudden urge to smash it, just to prove that she could change something. The light gleamed on the delicate blue glaze and she felt the wonderful shape in her hands. Carefully she set it down. But it is only because it is so beautiful, she told herself; I could do it if I wanted to. And she ran down the stairs after Jamie.

He was standing on the gravel outside, staring up at the house and trying to decide which was the right window. He calculated that it was the first room of the Victorian wing where fortunately the ivy had spread across from the old house. He tugged at the twisted stems to gauge their strength and then began to climb.

Lucy watched him anxiously. "Oh, Jamie, do be careful," she called. "It won't help at all if you break a leg."

But he reached the window without much difficulty and, peering in, found that he had indeed picked the right one.

Mrs Wickens, obviously in a state of shock, was lolling in a large armchair. There was a gin bottle on the table beside her and she had a full glass in her hand. Next to the bottle lay the ring of keys. If the window had been open, Jamie reckoned that he could have reached it, but as it was a chilly night and as the Victorians were not enthusiastic about fresh air, all the windows were tightly closed. Jamie felt desperate. He broke off a long twig of ivy and put it between his teeth in readiness. Then he reached in his pocket for his handkerchief and, winding it around his fist for protection, smashed the window pane.

He had guessed that the sound of breaking glass would bring the old woman to her feet but he had banked on being too quick for her. He would poke the ivy twig through the window, pull the key-ring within reach and be away down the ivy with it before she could do anything.

But he had only the one free hand and when he picked the twig from between his teeth he was hampered by the handkerchief. He fumbled wildly and the twig slipped from his grasp. He pulled at another one, but by the time he had broken it off, it was too late. Mrs Wickens, alternately shrieking "Ghosts!" and "Burglars!", was already dragging the heavy inside shutters across the window.

Disconsolately, he climbed down to the ground where Lucy stood waiting.

"Maybe you're right," he said. "Maybe we can't change anything. We were fools ever to come."

"Oh, don't say that." Lucy could not bear to see him in

despair. "It's only because it isn't the right time. When it is, Mr Blunden will come."

Even as Lucy spoke, there were footsteps on the gravel and they turned half expecting to see the old solicitor. But it was the big man and they stood very still, shrinking back instinctively into the shadow of the wall. As he passed by in the moonlight, they saw him glance furtively back over his shoulder.

"What do you think he gets up to?" whispered Lucy nervously. "He's always shuffling around in the darkness. Last time I saw him, he was carrying a great bundle of wood."

"I don't know." Jamie was not really interested. "I suppose Mrs Wickens makes him do all the dirty jobs around the place: fetch the coal and light the fires. He looks too stupid for anything else."

"Light the fires ... " His casual words seemed to click in Lucy's mind with something else: something which she had been aware of ever since she came out of the house, but which she had not really registered. She sniffed and sniffed again. Then she grabbed Jamie's arm.

"What is it?" he said, sensing her sudden fear.

"Smoke!" she said and they stared at each other not wanting to believe it.

"Quickly," said Jamie. He seized her hand and they ran along the gravel. As they reached the far end of the house, they saw that the library was already burning.

"I think the time has come," said Jamie bitterly. "Where is your Mr Blunden now?"

11

JAMIE'S first reaction to the fire was a cold feeling of panic, a feeling that he would not be able to cope with what was happening. Ghosts he had found intriguing, moving out of his own time was an exciting adventure. But now, reality seemed to have overtaken him without warning and there were two lives at stake.

He stared at the dark windows of the nursery, high up on the second floor. There was no sound, no sign of movement, and he wondered if Sara and Georgie had fallen asleep. He picked up a handful of gravel and threw it up towards the window. Most of it fell short, but a few small stones pattered against the blank glass. There was no response: they were obviously sleeping. The stump of candle would have burnt out long ago leaving them in the dark, and it would be hard to keep awake then.

Lucy was staring at him expectantly. "What can we do?" she asked anxiously. She felt somehow personally responsible for Mr Blunden's failure to appear.

Jamie considered the drainpipe. "I might be able to climb it," he began.

"Oh, no, you mustn't!" Lucy caught his arm. "Remember what happened to Tom when he climbed it. The sexton said ... "

"You mean, remember what *will* happen to Tom when he climbs it," Jamie corrected her.

Lucy looked confused; then she saw what he meant. "Of course," she said, "he is bound to come. You must stop him, Jamie."

"No," said Jamie gently but firmly, "*you* must stop him." He put his hands on her shoulders and looked her in the eye, trying somehow to put courage into her timid heart. "Listen," he told her, "we have got to separate for a while. I am going to the cellar to find an axe or something; since we can't get the keys I shall have to break down the nursery door. But someone must stay here to warn Tom and it has to be you. His life depends on it."

Lucy swallowed hard; she was beginning to feel sick. The whole thing was somehow going wrong. She had been so sure that Mr Blunden would come. She wondered if he could not come because Jamie had broken his promise to trust him. She felt certain that they could not do it alone. Jamie acted as though it was a simple matter of saving two children from a fire, forgetting that it had all happened a hundred years before. But Lucy knew that it was beyond their power to change the Pattern of the Wheel unaided.

She dreaded the thought of being alone again but she nodded and said, "I'll stay here. I'll see that Tom is all right."

"Good girl!" Jamie sighed with relief.

Lucy watched him go with a leaden heart. Suppose ... suppose she should never see him again.

It was nightmarish when he had gone. The wind was high and clouds were blowing up over the moon. Within the library the fire had taken a firm hold, eating its way greedily through the books and bookshelves.

If only we could run to the telephone, thought Lucy, struggling to keep her mind on commonplace things, and call up a large friendly fire-engine with hoses and turn-tables and burly, reassuring firemen. It came to her with something of a shock that her life and Jamie's were full of everyday marvels that would make Sara and Georgie gape with astonished disbelief. She stared up at the darkened window, and thought of the instant miracle of electric light ...

There were running footsteps in the night and out of nowhere Tom was suddenly beside her. His face was up-turned towards the high window and he had not noticed Lucy.

"Miss Sara, Miss Sara!" he called frantically. "Oh, Miss Sara, are you there?"

Lucy called his name but he was shouting too loudly to hear her. She ran forward and caught hold of his arm.

"Tom," she said, "it's me. Don't you remember? I'm Miss Sara's friend."

Catching Sara's name, he paused and peered at her in the dim light.

"Why, 'tis you, miss," he said. "Is Miss Sara all right? Is she safe then?"

"Not yet, she and Georgie are still in the nursery. But Jamie has gone to find an axe to break down the door."

" 'T'will be quicker by the drainpipe," he said. "I reckon they must be sleeping so I'll go on ahead and waken them."

"Oh, but you mustn't," Lucy told him, "you see the drainpipe is dangerous, you are sure to fall."

"Now don't you go fretting, miss," he said reassuringly, " 'tis a new building and them pipes is as safe as houses."

He moved away towards the wall.

Lucy ran after him. "But, Tom, it isn't safe, really it isn't! You will fall and be killed; I know you will."

Tom tried to be patient with her.

"Now, see here, miss," he said and he thumped the big square drainpipe with his fist, "don't that sound strong enough? Why, this part of the house weren't built above fifteen years back."

Lucy had to admit that it did seem to be quite sound, but that only made her task harder. Tom had already taken hold of the pipe and was looking for a foothold.

She grew desperate. "Oh, please don't, Tom. Really, you mustn't. I just know that you will be killed if you do. I can't explain how I know, but believe me, I do!"

He paused a moment and the moon lit up his face as he looked at her kindly. "Happen I shall be killed," he said simply, "but there's some as a person would gladly die for. Miss Sara has been everything to me. There's not another soul in the world has a kind word for me, but Miss Sara ... she's so gentle, and she's teaching me to read and write. Oh, 'tis hard to explain, miss, but she's in danger now and if I knew as certain as tomorrow that I should break my neck, why, 'twouldn't stop me trying to save her."

Lucy groaned and buried her face in her hands as he began to climb.

We can't change anything, she thought. I wish we had never, never, come. I don't want to see it all happen.

She forced herself to look up at Tom, stepping back to see him more clearly.

"It won't help Sara if you are killed!" she called angrily. "You will only make things worse."

She covered her eyes again, dreading to see him slip and fall.

If only that awful potion would wear off, she thought, and I could find myself back beside the sundial. If only Mr Blunden would come. If only there was something I could do!

A loud, harsh voice jerked her back to reality, and she saw the big man standing not six feet away from her.

"You come down, you sneaking brat!" he growled. "I'll not 'ave you meddling."

But Tom was out of reach, climbing steadily up the pipe which, to Lucy's relief, seemed steady enough.

"I'll 'ave you down off there, you little varmint!" The big man raised his hand and waved what looked like a heavy iron poker. He thrust it between the pipe and the wall and began to pull on it, grunting and groaning in the effort to force them apart.

It was a moment or two before Lucy realized what he was doing. She remembered with a gasp of dismay that the old sexton had only guessed that the pipe had been weak. No one could have known when the fire was over and the broken body was found, that the gardener's boy had not died accidentally.

Instinctively, she began to call for Jamie, but she soon

realized that it was useless. For once she would have to act by herself.

Without pausing to consider the consequences, she rushed at the big man and, seizing the back of his jacket, began to worry at it like a determined terrier tackling an angry bull. She was too small to budge him but he was momentarily distracted. He turned with a roar and though he saw nothing, he struck out with his fist into the darkness. Lucy felt a blow that knocked her sideways and she fell heavily on to the gravel path.

When she staggered to her feet again, with her hands and her knees bruised and sore, the big man had resumed his attack on the drainpipe, but Tom was almost at the top. Lucy saw him reach out, feeling for a hand-hold, but the window was shut.

Lucy shouted to Sara to open it but it remained dark and blank, the heavy curtains unmoving. She wondered how they could possibly sleep through so much noise and confusion.

With a hoarse grunt of triumph, the big man wrenched the bottom end of the pipe away from the wall, but Tom had grasped the window sill and was painfully hauling himself up.

"Sara, Miss Sara!" Lucy heard him call. "For pity's sake, miss, open the window."

The big man rocked the drainpipe from side to side but found it impossible to dislodge the gardener's boy. He paused, muttering angrily to himself, and seemed to consider what to do next. Then he snorted, picked up the poker again, and stepped back a little way. Lucy saw the gleam of broken teeth as he smiled and a look of cunning stole across his face.

Then his arm went back and, with a sudden lunge, he sent the heavy poker flying through the air towards the nursery window.

Lucy couldn't bear to see what followed.

She hid her face in her hands, but she could not keep out Tom's sudden cry of pain or the crashing thud in the bushes below the window.

12

WHEN Jamie left Lucy, it was not without misgivings.

He knew that she would be very nervous alone, that it would not be easy for her to wait patiently in the wind-moaning, owl-haunted night. But he also knew that she had her own sort of courage, not the kind that acts boldly, but the kind that endures. Lucy would not desert her post, of that he was certain, and, safe in the knowledge that Tom would be all right, he turned his full attention to the problem of Sara and Georgie.

Once inside the house, it took him a minute or two to get his bearings. But he found the cellar door unlocked and went down into the darkness, fumbling for a light switch until he remembered that there was none. What a fool I was not to bring a torch, he thought, I might have known I should need one. He felt in his pockets and among the useful oddments without which he never felt dressed, he found a tattered book of matches. As he tore one out, his fingers told him that there were only two there.

I mustn't strike one, he thought, until I know what I'm looking for. I want the coal-cellar, the one where Georgie was. There will be a chopper in there for splitting fire-wood.

He knew from the garden grating that this cellar would

be by the outside wall, but he had lost his sense of direction on the winding stairs. He felt his way around the clammy walls, until he found a passage leading away. Then he struck his first match with care, and was rewarded with the glimpse of a door at the end of the passage. The brief light faded to a red glow between his fingers. He dropped the spent stub and hurrying through the darkness, pushed open the door.

A shaft of moonlight shone through the grating, and his heart leaped as he saw it gleam on a bright axe. The blade had been sunk deep into a log of wood by a strength far greater than his own. He seized it and pulled, but it was like trying to get the sword Excalibur out of the stone. In desperation he raised both axe and log high in the air and brought them down on to the floor with all his might. The axe rang clear on the cold stone as the split log fell apart.

Panting a little, he glanced around for anything else that might be useful. The moonlight caught the glass of a lamp hanging from the roof. He lifted it down carefully and opened it, and finding that the wick smelled of oil, he chanced his last match. The flame flared and then dulled to a soft yellow glow which lit up the dark corners of the cellar and showed him a coil of rope hanging behind the door.

There was no time to lose. Slinging the rope over his shoulder, he took the axe in one hand and the lamp in the other, and went back along the passage, but the axe was heavy, the lamp was awkward to hold, and the coil of rope kept slipping. He could see no further than the pool of light he carried, and he thought longingly of electric light and powerful, straight-beamed torches.

The sound of the fire grew louder as he reached the ground floor and made his way towards the stairs. It was a dull, gnawing noise with here and there a loud crack like the snapping of bones, as if the house were being swiftly devoured by some giant animal. As he walked resolutely towards it, he felt that he was walking into the animal's den.

If I read about this in a book, he thought it would seem like a bold, heroic exploit. But in fact, I'm only doing it because I can't think of any alternative. He could not even run to the rescue as people did in stories; he was too burdened by lamp and axe and rope to do more than plod doggedly up the stairs.

The smoke was growing thicker, and the bright circle of lamplight had contracted to a dim blur on the surrounding darkness. Worse than car headlamps in a fog, he thought gloomily.

There was something uncanny about the quietness of it all. A fire should be a scene of noise and confusion, bells ringing, people shouting, not this steady low roaring in the night. And why no sound from the nursery above? He was on the last flight of stairs now and had expected cries of alarm, fists pounding on the door, not this disturbing silence. A terrible suspicion seized him: he had read that most people in fires died of suffocation and the rising smoke grew thicker as he reached the top of the house ... The thought was unbearable and, reaching the landing, he broke into a run. Outside the nursery, he set down the lamp and dropping the rope and the axe, hammered upon the door.

"Sara!" he called. "Sara! Georgie! Are you all right?"
But there was only silence from the room beyond.

131

The door was stout and Jamie realized that he was wasting time. He gripped the axe in both hands and began to hack at the wood. It was not as easy as he had thought. Unlike the doors in films which are made of thin wood for the hero to destroy at a blow, this was of solid oak. If the axe came down with too much force, it bit deep into the wood and stuck there, so that he had to spend valuable seconds wiggling it up and down to loosen it.

A fit of coughing brought on by the dense smoke made him helpless for a minute or two, and he realized with a growing sense of urgency that he might well be overcome before the door was open. I ought to lie on the floor, he thought: the air is always clearer near the ground because the smoke rises. But what was the use of knowing all the sensible things to do in a fire, if you were too busy hacking down a door to bother with them?

He raised the axe angrily, and much to his relief, felt the wood splinter as it went through. But that was only the beginning. There was no key on the inside to be turned by stretching his hand through the hole. Before the door would open, he must cut out the lock completely.

He felt sick with the smoke he had swallowed and the fits of coughing that tore at his lungs. But the door was weakening. All at once, without warning, it gave way under a particularly heavy blow, so that he was caught off balance and stumbled forward into the room. The falling axe missed his foot by a fraction.

He turned back for the lamp and as the light fell inside the room, he saw with a rush of thankfulness that the well-fitted door had kept out the smoke. Now, however, it came billowing in, forming a blanket of darkness above his head. He turned hastily to slam the door and stood leaning against it, breathing the clearer air and trying to get some strength back.

In the corner of the room, just beyond the circle of the light, he could see Sara with her arm round Georgie, lying on the bed. Through all the splintering crashes of the axe on the door they had not stirred, and yet with no smoke, they could not have suffocated. He picked up the lamp and moved wearily across the room, half afraid to reach them. Suppose they were dead? Suppose the fire had been meant only to cover up a murder which had already taken place? And yet, they looked so peaceful as though they had simply fallen asleep.

He stood gazing down at them. He half stretched out his hand to touch them, but he was afraid that he might find them cold.

I was wrong, he thought, I haven't changed anything. It wasn't possible for me alone, I should have trusted the old man, and now it is too late. However hard I try, there is always something I have not bargained for.

And then a tiny movement caught his eye. He held his breath, staring at the pillow where a strand of Sara's long, dark hair was moving gently. It lay an inch or two from George's face and he realized with a surge of joy that the little boy was breathing. He reached out his hand and grasping Sara's arm, shook it roughly.

"Sara!" he said. "Sara, wake up!"

But she lay quite still.

He put the lamp down on a near-by table and seizing her

with both hands pulled her up into a sitting position. Her head fell forward and her steady breathing grew a little louder.

Jamie stared at her for a moment in disbelief. It was ridiculous that anyone should sleep so heavily, especially in a burning house. He shook her and called her name urgently, but she slept on. It was almost, he thought crossly, as though she had been drugged ... And then it all became clear to him: Bella and the mugs of hot milk, Mrs Wickens alone in the passage, holding the empty tray and laughing. She had given the children something to make certain they did not wake during the fire and devise some means for their own escape.

He lowered Sara on to the pillow and stood for a moment baffled by this unexpected frustration.

But before he could think what to do, a sudden cry rang out.

"Sara! Miss Sara!"

It was very close at hand and coming, unlikely as it seemed, from just outside the window. In a moment he was across the room, pulling aside the heavy curtain. A tense, white face stared in from the darkness outside. Jamie struggled with the catch and threw up the window to find Tom staring up at him. His hands were strained to skin and bone as he clung to the window sill.

Without pausing to consider how or why he was there, Jamie leaned out and catching hold of him by the back of his jacket, hauled him inside. As he did so, Tom cried out and something struck the wall by the window with a clang and fell noisily into the bushes below. Glancing swiftly down, Jamie saw Lucy, her head buried in her hands, and the big man, snarling angrily as he stared up at them.

There was no time to speculate on what had happened. Tom lay in a heap on the floor trying to get his breath, and as Jamie crouched down beside him, he gasped, "Miss Sara ... is she ... all right?"

"They're alive," said Jamie, "but they seem to have been drugged. It's a good thing you're here," he went on, "because we're going to have to carry them down the stairs."

Tom scrambled to his feet and let out a yelp of pain.

"What is it?" asked Jamie anxiously.

"That Mr Wickens threw something at me. It caught my ankle and 'tis a bit damaged like."

"Can you walk?"

"Oh, I'll walk all right if 'tis to get Miss Sara out." His voice was bluff and confident but, seeing his face twist with pain, Jamie had his doubts.

He crossed to the door and opened it. As he did so there was a rush of wind and the flames leaped higher. He closed it again quickly and turned to Tom. "It's the window," he said, "it's making a terrible draught. We must shut it or the stairwell will be like a giant chimney."

The gardener's boy limped over to the window and wrestled with the sash. When it was safely closed, Jamie said, "There's no point in opening the door again before we have to, it only lets the smoke in. Now the first thing is to find some water and damp a cloth."

Tom looked bewildered. "But 'tis wasting time ... " he began.

Jamie was tearing wide strips off one of the sheets. "You

haven't been through the smoke," he said. "It's suffocating out there; we'd never make it without something over our mouths."

Tom found a copper water jug and turned it upside down. "Not a drop," he said mournfully.

Jamie cast around frantically. In one corner there was a small vase of wilted daffodils; he threw them out and with a mixed feeling of relief and repugnance, found a few inches of stale green water.

Damping the cloths, he tied one each over the faces of the sleeping children and showed Tom how to tie one over his own mouth and nose.

"Now," he said, his voice muffled by the foul-smelling cloth, "let's get them out of here as fast as we can."

"I'll take Miss Sara," said Tom.

It seemed sensible since the gardener's boy was bigger and stronger, but Jamie wondered about the weakened ankle. However there was no time to argue and he was about to hoist young Georgie across his shoulder when the door burst open behind them. It hit the wall with a shuddering crash, Tom gave a cry of dismay, and Jamie turned to see the big man. He stood in the doorway with the poker in one hand and an expression of scorn on his face.

"Did yer think you 'ad me beat then?" he sneered at Tom. "Did yer think I'd let yer play the 'ero, and spoil everything now?"

Tom was standing in front of Sara. "You'll not touch her," he said. "You'll not lay a finger on either of them!" His eyes flickered from side to side as he searched for a weapon. Then he stooped suddenly beyond the ring of light and as he straightened up the lamplight gleamed on the edge of a blade. He faced the big man with the axe in his hands and his voice trembled a little; "I'll kill you," he said, "before you shall touch her."

Jamie's stomach turned over. He stared from one to the other, from the gardener's boy, cold with resolution and fear of what he might have to do, grasping the great axe with its icy blade, to the big man framed by the flames and the billowing smoke with the iron poker in his hand.

A momentary fear gleamed in the man's eyes as he saw the axe. He stepped backwards, taken by surprise, and lurched sideways against the doorpost. Jamie saw that he was drunk. He ran to Tom's side, "You can't kill him!" he said. "He doesn't know what he's doing."

"I'm not minded to kill him if I can help it," said Tom, "though he well deserves it. But I'll keep his eyes off you while you drag Sara and Georgie out. Now get back into the shadows where he can't see you."

It was hardly the moment, thought Jamie, to explain that the big man could not see him anywhere, but he was grateful for the freedom it gave him.

Tom moved forward into the circle of lamplight while Jamie edged round in the shadows behind him. He decided to take Sara first while he had most strength and, cautiously, he began to drag her towards the door. As he did so she stirred slightly and he saw a gleam of hope. He remembered that when people were drugged you had to walk them up and down to revive them. So he changed his hold on Sara, grasping her round the waist and throwing one of her arms across his shoulder. At first her feet dragged along the floor, but then he felt her take a few stumbling steps. As they reached the door, the big man lunged towards Tom and they were able to pass behind him unseen, out into the thick smoke on the stairs.

Jamie could hear the heavy trampling of feet and once the awful clash of steel on steel. But the shout that followed was more a grunt of frustration than a cry of pain and he dared not pause to look back.

Sara was now carrying some of her own weight and though her steps were uncontrolled, Jamie found that he could guide her without too much difficulty. As they reached the top of the stairs, she tried to speak but her voice was muffled by the wet cloth.

"It's all right," he mumbled back, and his mouth was filled with the taste of wet daffodils.

She raised her head a little and he saw her eyes move searchingly above the white mask. Then he made out what she was saying. It was, "Georgie?"

He had to lie. He hated it, but he knew that if he told her that her brother was still up there, she might fight to go back.

"He's safe," he told her but his words were drowned by a crash from above, followed by a string of oaths. "Safe!" he repeated. "Now do come on!"

Sara seemed to accept his assurance without question, which made him feel worse in a way. But I will come back for him, he promised her silently. I'll see that he is safe. And he struggled on, step by step, keeping close to the wall for the flames were creeping up the well in the centre.

As they started on the last flight, he heard steps on the

stairs above, and glanced up anxiously, afraid that they might be pursued. But he could see only dark figures moving in the dense smoke and then a sudden gleam of flames on the axe blade as it struck the banister rail. He tore his eyes away. If he could only get Sara safely outside, he could go back and help Tom somehow. She was walking more easily now as they reached the bottom of the stairs. The fire was burning fiercely a little way along the passage that led to the library, but the smoke was less dense now that they were at ground level. Panting for breath, he half carried Sara the last few yards to the outer door and flung it open. With a roar the wind swept in and they stumbled through into the blessedly clean, damp coolness of the night.

He realized that the wind was a terrible threat to those still inside so he let Sara slip to the ground and turned to close the door. He knew that he had to go in again, but he also knew that unless he paused to fill his lungs with clean air, he might never make it.

He pulled the now blackened cloth from his mouth and drew a deep breath. Even as he did so, he heard a cry of joy through the dark night and Lucy came running.

"Oh, Jamie," she said, "I thought you'd never come!"

"I have ... to go ... back," he gasped.

"Oh, Jamie, you can't."

"It's Georgie," he panted, "and Tom ... got to help."

"But Jamie ... "

"Look after Sara," and before she could stop him, he had pulled the mask up over his face and plunged back into the building, closing the door behind him.

The first thing that met his eyes was the body of the big

man. He lay at the bottom of the stairwell and it was obvious that he had fallen. It was equally obvious from the grotesque position in which he lay that he was dead.

Jamie ran up the stairs calling to Tom but there was no answer. He found him at the bottom of the second flight, his head and shoulders on the landing, his legs sprawling untidily upwards. He was quite still. Jamie uttered a silent prayer as he bent over him and could have shouted with joy when he found that the gardener's boy was still breathing.

I ought not to move him, he thought, in case there are broken bones, but I can't leave him here. As gently as he could, he grasped Tom under the arms and eased him along the landing to the lower stairs. He was much heavier than Sara, and Jamie could only drag him by moving backwards, feeling blindly for each step as he went.

He saw with dismay that the banisters were already burning. Fierce tongues of flame licked along them and the brown varnished wood first blazed and then blackened. His heart sank as he realized that he had yet another trip to make, that Georgie was still trapped in the nursery above.

I must not think of it, he told himself. I must concentrate on what I am doing.

They had reached the bottom of the stairs and now, at every step, they drew a little nearer to the door and the life-giving air beyond it. Three more steps ... two more ... one. He lowered Tom gently to the floor and turned the handle of the door. The sweet air roared in around them and the stairs seemed to explode into flames.

He found Lucy outside with Sara leaning against her.

When she saw Tom, the older girl gave a cry and knelt down beside him.

"Oh, Tom!" She put out a hand to touch him. "Is he all right?"

"I think so. He's alive anyway." Jamie straightened up and rubbed his hand wearily over his blackened face. His eyes were sore from the heat, his eyeballs dry, his eyelids scratchy.

"But where is Georgie?" Sara seemed suddenly to remember him. She looked up at Jamie. "Is he still up there?" Her eyes grew wild and she stared up at the nursery window. She rose to her feet but stumbled and Lucy had to steady her. "I must get Georgie!" she protested.

"It's all right," said Jamie, with a confidence he was far from feeling, "I'm going to fetch him now." Ignoring Lucy's cry of dismay, he turned and, taking one last gulp of cool air, he went back into the burning house.

Left behind in the garden where the leaping flames made monstrous shadows among the tossing branches of the trees, Lucy tried hard to be calm and strong. She drew a deep breath and fought down the urge to scream. She forced herself to turn her back on the house, to help Sara to drag Tom across the gravel on to the lawn.

And so it was that she did not see the dark figure of a horseman who came galloping up the drive, the broken carriage traces trailing behind him. The crunch of the children's feet on the gravel, and the roaring of the fire drowned the sound of the horse's hooves and the man's stifled cry of dismay. He slid to the ground and ran towards the burning building with the awkward gait of a man who is no longer young. In a moment he had passed into the house, and the heavy door slammed shut behind him.

The horse panicked at the sight of the flames and cantered away into the windy darkness.

13

JAMIE had known even as he closed the door behind him that it was impossible, and yet he had not turned back.

It's all my fault, he thought, for thinking I could do it alone. Lucy was right: I'm not just trying to save two children, I'm trying to change the Pattern of the Wheel. Mr Blunden said it could only be changed if he suffered instead, but now he is not here and there is only me.

He stared at the staircase; the carpet was blazing and the flames had begun to devour the wooden treads. I can't walk through it, he thought desperately, my shoes would burn and my clothes ... and coming back it would be even worse. He remembered the rope. The fire might not be so bad upstairs, it might be possible to lower Georgie from the window, he would not be so very heavy, not like Tom or Sara. If it was only possible to get up there.

He talked to himself reassuringly as if to a frightened horse; as if by persuading himself that he could do it, it would become possible. After all, he argued, I'm not even here really: this is all happening a hundred years ago. I'm not even born yet, so how can the fire hurt me?

Half-convinced, he took a deep breath and moved towards the inferno. But the heat met him like a glowing wall and beat him back before he even reached the flames.

I can't do it, he admitted at last, it isn't possible. Whether or not I have the courage, I just cannot walk into those flames and come out alive.

Desolation filled him, a terrible feeling of helplessness. Tears stung his eyes and involuntarily he cried out, "I would if I could! Don't you see that it just isn't possible!" as if the sleeping child accused him.

A voice beside him said "Take my hand" and, turning incredulously, he saw the tall figure of Mr Blunden not thin and wraithlike but real and solid beside him.

"We will go together," said the old man, "and the fire will not touch you. It is not your fault, it is not your punishment, and it will not harm you. It will take all your courage for the flames will surround you and the floor will burn under your feet, but while you hold my hand, you will feel nothing."

Jamie stared at him and fought against the doubt in his mind. If only I had not seen him that last time, he thought, if I could only think of him as good and kind ...

"... it would be easier to trust him," the old man finished the sentence which had been spoken only inside Jamie's head. "That is what you were thinking?"

Jamie nodded miserably.

The old man sighed. "Alas," he said, "it was not meant to be easy. To change the Pattern of the Wheel: it is not an easy thing. You must trust me not because of what I am, but in spite of it."

"I think I understand now," said Jamie.

Mr Blunden held out his hand. "It is an act of faith," he said gently. "It is your trust that is necessary and your courage but not your suffering. Only you can act, but only I shall suffer."

Jamie took the old man's hand and it was cold as spring water.

"It is time." Mr Blunden's voice was strangely joyful. "Look straight ahead of you," he said, "and do not be afraid."

Jamie looked straight ahead of him and together they walked towards the fire. As they drew near the wall of heat, Jamie felt the edges of his mind shrivel in anticipation and yet he passed into the fire and felt nothing.

He lifted his feet and put them down on blazing carpet and crackling wood and his shoes, brown leather and rather muddy, remained unscorched. He grasped the burning stair-rail with his free hand but the skin stayed smooth and unblistered.

He realized that coolness was flowing into him from Mr Blunden's hand and a wild excitement filled him. Forgetting the old man's injunction to look straight ahead, he turned saying, "It's incredible, I can't feel a thing," but the words dried in his mouth at the sight of the old lawyer's face. Though the fire had not touched it, it was twisted with pain, and Jamie realized with a shudder that just as the coolness flowed into him from Mr Blunden's hand, so the pain that he could not feel flowed back into the old man.

"Look ... straight ... ahead!" The words came like a gasp and Jamie tore his eyes away. He stared upwards at the burning stairs and walked on, drained of feeling.

The flames were not so fierce on the second flight of stairs. Even the thick smoke seemed unreal. Jamie found that he could breathe in and out as easily as though he were in the garden outside, and he tried to close his ears to the sound of the old man coughing.

Georgie lay on the bed still sleeping soundly. Because he was much smaller than Sara, the drug had affected him more deeply and he made no movement as Jamie lifted him and slung him over his shoulder. To do this he needed both hands and he was forced to release Mr Blunden's hand for a moment. As soon as he did so, the choking smoke seemed to fill his lungs and the heat of the room brought him out in a sudden sweat.

He turned quickly and, taking hold again, moved with the old man towards the stairs. This time he knew better than to glance at his companion. He concentrated his attention on the problem of balancing Georgie over his shoulder. The strange immunity from harm seemed to envelop both of them, and as they reached the last flight of stairs where the fire was fiercest, Jamie moved into the flames without flinching. They roared and sucked about the woodwork, the carpet had quite vanished and the wooden steps were like glowing firewood, split and twisted and with all the substance gone out of them. And yet it did not occur to Jamie that they might not bear his weight.

He moved as if in an enchanted circle, as if he were freed entirely from the laws of nature. And so, he was thrown completely off balance when the weakened wood crumbled beneath his feet.

There was a strange singing in his ears, an unaccountable dizziness in his head. With no time to think, he acted instinctively. Tearing his hand from the old solicitor's grasp,

146

he threw both arms around the unconscious child to protect him as best he could. Then he fell helplessly towards the flames.

The two girls in the windy garden were kneeling beside Tom, wiping his face with handkerchiefs damped in the dew-wet grass.

"Do you think he'll be all right?" asked Lucy, staring anxiously at his still form.

"I think so," said Sara. "His arm may be broken, I fear, and his ankle is badly swollen. But he breathes steadily and his face is warm."

"And what about you?"

"Oh, I have suffered little harm," Sara laughed shakily. "I have a terrible headache, but that is a small price to pay for one's life."

She moistened the handkerchief again and laid it gently across Tom's forehead. "We owe so much to your brother," she went on. "Although he is quite safe in Mr Blunden's care, yet the courage needed is very great and I think ... "

Lucy had turned very pale. "Mr Blunden didn't come," she blurted out, "Jamie went alone."

Sara's hands were suddenly still. She turned her face slowly up and the grey eyes stared disbelievingly at Lucy.

"He has gone back alone?" she said.

Miserably Lucy nodded. "He said he didn't think he could trust Mr Blunden after the way he treated you, that he would save you by himself. He said he would be all right," she added lamely.

"But it is like a furnace in there! And I sent him back in again."

Sara dropped the handkerchief and scrambled to her feet. "I must go after him," she said and began to run towards the house. But the drug had weakened her and before she had gone halfway, she crumpled and fell.

In a moment, Lucy was crouching beside her.

"I'm all right," Sara's voice was shaky and uncertain, "but my legs are weak. Oh, Lucy, we must try to help him. He is very brave, but so foolish to go alone."

"I'll go," said Lucy quickly. "I'll go and see if I can find him."

"Please hurry," Sara clasped her hand anxiously. "I would do anything in the world to save Georgie, but I would not sacrifice both of them."

Lucy squeezed her hand but there was nothing she could say. She turned and ran towards the house and as she did so she heard a crashing sound from within. She forced the door open and the heat streamed out at her as if from an oven. Georgie lay a few feet inside the door, but beyond him the stairs had gone, only a mass of charred and twisted timbers remained.

Great sobs began to force their way through Lucy. "Oh, Jamie, Jamie," she said again and again. But even as she wept, she was gathering up the small boy who was unmarked, unharmed, and apparently sleeping.

She turned her back on the flames and went slowly out through the door, but grief was tearing her apart. She felt sick and light-headed and strangely thin, as if all that happened was no longer real.

She reached Sara and as she did, she let the limp form in her arms slip to the ground. She thought that Sara spoke to her, but she felt so ill, she could not hear or answer. Dimly she was aware of horses' hooves and carriage wheels, of voices crying out. She shook her head in an effort to clear it, and out of the darkness she saw the children's uncle running towards the house. His face was white, his round eyes staring, and he seemed to be shouting, but she could not tell whether it was for the children or for Bella that he feared. She could see no sign of the old lawyer.

She raised her voice accusingly, "You are too late!" she shouted. "You are always too late..." but her words seemed to die on the passing wind.

The roaring of the fire filled her ears like the waves of the sea. Her head began to spin, faster and faster, it was like a giant whirlpool and she realized suddenly what was happening.

"Not without Jamie!" she screamed. "I won't go back without Jamie!" But the scream was silent and everything grew dark.

When the darkness cleared, she was lying across the seat by the sundial and she was alone. The cold stone against her cheek felt very real, and raising her head, she saw that it was a little after sunset. The last fading light in the sky caught the tops of the high trees and shone on the creeper-covered ruins of the library. It was very quiet; only a faint movement of wind among the leaves and distant owl-noises.

She felt as if she had just woken from a particularly unpleasant dream, but had forgotten the details.

Well, I don't think I want to remember, she thought, although it might have been fun to tell Jamie.

And then it all came rushing back and she knew that it had not been a dream. With a cry of fear, she sprang to her feet and ran towards the ruins. Somewhere in there Jamie must be, if he was not altogether lost in the far distances of Time.

She stumbled through the tall weeds and the all-consuming creepers. Nothing remained where the door had been but beyond there was a high decaying wall beside a broken archway. And Jamie lay still in a small, crumpled heap at the foot of the wall.

Part Four

~~~~~~

14

LUCY sat on the woodland stile, deep in thought. Bees droned and skimmed through the warm air and the scent of rotting mould was underlined by the pungent smell of bluebell leaves thrusting up towards the light. It was a good day for just sitting and breathing but Lucy's mind was on other things. She was trying to decide whether she should go on or go back.

It was Easter Sunday morning, nearly two days now. The memory of Jamie, lying still and silent against the white sheets, was like a dull pain inside her.

A bad fall, the doctor had said, difficult to tell if there was damage to the brain without a long, rough journey to the hospital ... unwilling to move him in his present state ... he may regain consciousness within the next twenty-four hours but if not ... He had peered into Jamie's eyes, shining a thin beam of light, and then frowned. Almost as though he had been drugged, he had muttered, more like a trance than a concussion ... The whole thing was very strange, very strange, not least the way the hair was singed on one side of the head.

I should have told him, thought Lucy, I should have told

him that Jamie is lost somewhere in Time, somewhere we cannot reach him, and all because Mr Blunden was not there.

But what would have been the use? She sighed. Almost certainly he would not have believed her and would have thought her heartless to make a game of her brother's accident. Even if he did believe me, she thought, what could he do? I don't suppose even the most up-to-date hospitals are equipped with Time machines.

What could anyone do? Their mother had said, "There is nothing we can do but pray," and she had dispatched Lucy to the Easter service to say prayers for all of them. But it was really only to get me out of the house, she thought, away from all the reminders of a celebration none of us can face. She thought of the flowers she had arranged so carefully, the chocolate Easter eggs that lay untouched, the presents that no one had the heart to open.

She swung her feet idly, kicking the rail of the stile. I could have prayed at home, she thought; I could even sit here by myself and pray all morning and God might hear me better without all the others around me, praying for something different.

But she had not argued with her mother, for it had suddenly seemed that if there was any answer to be found, she would find it in the quiet grey stones of the churchyard.

For the first ten minutes she had run all the way along the footpath that switchbacked through fields of sprouting corn. But at the edge of the wood she had paused, short of breath and with a stitch in her side, and now that she had recovered, she was afraid to go on.

Suppose nothing had changed? And yet, how *could*

anything be changed? Imagine the vicar's astonishment, the outcry from the sexton, if they arrived one morning to find that one of the graves had disappeared ... two really, although if Tom's was not marked, perhaps they would not notice the difference. It was just not possible to make grave-stones vanish. Once in London, when she was very young, she had tried to move a mountain, though it was only a small hill really. She had sat in church listening earnestly to a sermon about faith moving mountains, and she had de-cided to move Highgate Hill. But though she had screwed up her eyes and covered her ears in an ecstasy of concentra-tion, her faith had moved nothing.

I can't still be as silly as that, she thought. I'm not a child any longer. I can't really go racing up to the churchyard expecting to find an empty patch of lawn or a yawning hole surrounded by a crowd of astonished villagers.

And yet, she thought desperately, if it is all just the same, what does it mean? Did we dream it, and if so, where is Jamie? not the pale, still, silent figure in the bed at home, but the real Jamie. If only he were here, he would know what to do. But that's silly, because if he were, there wouldn't be any problem. Her mind buzzed and darted as confusingly as the small striped flies which hovered around her on wings of moving air.

She tried to decide what Jamie would do if he were sitting on the stile and she were lying in bed. *He* would go straight up to the churchyard and look, she told herself, but then he is braver than I am.

Nevertheless, she climbed down from the stile and began to walk resolutely up the hill through the trees. The steady sound of the bell flowed down to meet her and when she reached the churchyard, the last of the congregation were disappearing into the ivy-covered porch. A flapping verger came hurrying round the corner and hustled her inside. The smart hats rose in unison like a flock of startled butterflies, and the first hymn was under way.

Jesus Christ is risen today,
Alleluia!

Lucy sang instinctively, and her gloom seemed to lighten as the words and the music bore her up. She tried hard to keep her mind on the service, and though it kept drifting back to the silent bed and the grey leaning stone, yet something of the joy of Easter came through to her. She prayed hard for Jamie and when she rose from her knees she felt strangely comforted. The service drew to a close, and she was tempted to hurry home without looking at the gravestone. But it seemed like a challenge, as if by going to see it, she declared her belief that what had happened had been real, and her faith that everything might still be well.

She slipped out of her pew while the bright hats were still hesitating reverently, and hurried round to the back of the churchyard. It was very quiet and the grey stones stood above their offerings of bright daffodils as if they had been there before even the church itself. The smooth turf still lay like a vast blanket over the hummocks of the sleepers beneath. Nothing had been disturbed; nothing had changed.

Lucy tried to remember exactly where the grave had been. She knew that there was a seat opposite, and that it was somewhere on the right-hand side not far from a spreading yew-tree. It should be about here, she thought, stopping by a broken column which looked familiar. She glanced around and a carved death's head grinned up at her. It leaped up in her memory and she hurried on to the next grave only to find a tall, remarkably ugly monument in pink-veined marble.

I've obviously got it wrong, she thought. The graveyard must be full of carved skulls and broken columns. She cast about for some remembered feature that would guide her. In any case, it's no use, she told herself, it's obvious that nothing has changed, nothing is missing. Jamie was right, you can't change what is already past, just as I couldn't break the blue vase. And yet ... she hesitated, torn between going and staying, and as she did so, she noticed the inscription carved on the pink monument:

THE GOOD SHEPHERD

GIVETH HIS LIFE

FOR THE SHEEP

Her eyes blurred without warning as the words brought back the memory of Jamie. If he died, she thought, no one would ever know that he had been trying to save Sara and Georgie. No one would put up a memorial to him with a tribute carved upon pink marble. They would think he had died foolishly climbing the wall in some childish prank. She stared angrily at the over-decorated monument;

FREDERICK PERCIVAL BLUNDEN

who gave his life to save

the children in his care

Lucy's heart seemed to miss a beat. She swallowed hard

155

and glanced nervously at the date below. Yesterday, she thought, but a hundred years ago! She looked frantically around for the children's small grey stone, but it was not there. She fought off a panicky feeling of unreality and hurried away along the gravel path. When I feel a bit better, she thought, I'll walk back and it will be the same as it was yesterday because it can't be different, it just isn't possible.

But when she had regained her composure and returned past the broken column and the carved death's head, the pink memorial was still there. Her knees felt weak. She sat down suddenly on a seat near by and stared disbelievingly. It *is* possible to change the past, she thought; Jamie did it. The children's grave had gone because they did not die, and the monument is here because Mr Blunden did. And that means that he *was* there and Jamie wasn't alone after all. She felt a glimmer of hope.

It was now perfectly clear to her what had happened, but her mind boggled at the thought of what other people would make of it. Suddenly, overnight in a small country churchyard a small grey gravestone had vanished and a massive marble monument had appeared in its place. Perhaps no one else has noticed it yet, she thought; perhaps it will cause a terrible commotion when they find out, with pictures in the papers and the churchyard full of television cameras.

She stared at the pink monstrosity with a sinking heart: she felt personally responsible for it. Suppose they should ask her to explain? She wished that Jamie were with her; he would know what to say. She rose to her feet, suddenly reluctant to be caught looking at it. She had a feeling that there were terrible penalties for tampering with gravestones.

She had once read in the paper about someone digging up a churchyard, something about sacrilege, or blasphemy, or even worse, witchcraft. Yes, that was it, something about black magic. She felt certain that whatever she and Jamie had done, it was not black magic, but would anyone believe her if she had to tell them about the ghosts and the brewing of the potion? She pictured the sour, disbelieving face of the magistrate. What would the penalties be for black magic? The boy next door in Camden Town had been sent away "in need of care and protection" for something far less awful than spiriting away gravestones.

She glared at the hated monument and groaned. "It's so big," she said aloud, "and so ugly. No one could fail to notice it."

She jumped about a foot in the air as a hand fell on her shoulder and the vicar's pleasant voice said cheerfully, "I'm afraid the Victorians were over-fond of the gaudier aspects of grief. Give me a simple grey headstone any day."

Lucy took this as a personal reproach and she said apologetically, "I suppose it must have been rather a shock to you."

The vicar smiled. "Well, I wouldn't put it as strongly as that, though I did wince a little when I first saw it. But during the ten years or so since I've been here, I seem to have grown rather fond of it. And you know, the old gentleman it commemorates was a rather wonderful person.

"Many years ago, there was a terrible fire up at the Old House where you are living now, and two children were trapped there. The old man was their guardian and he had been to dine at the house. As he was being driven home, the carriage broke down and looking back the old man saw the flames in the distance. He seized one of the horses and rode headlong back to the house. Rushing into the burning building, he saved the little boy, but the strain must have been too much for the old man for he collapsed and died."

Lucy stared at the marble monument. "Then it has always been there?" she said stupidly.

The vicar looked at her curiously. "For about a hundred years," he said.

Lucy thought about it. "Perhaps I'm in the wrong place," she said. "I was looking for a little grey stone."

"Well now, we have a great many of those. Do you by any chance know the inscription?"

Lucy hesitated and a strange uncertainty took hold of her. The vicar seemed to see nothing wrong with his churchyard. Her common sense told her that the monument had been there all the time, that she just hadn't noticed it before. And yet, it was so very noticeable. Then she thought, If we have really changed the past, then the monument *would* have been here all the time, and the children's grave would not have been here at all. But at the same time, she and Jamie had seen it, or rather not at the same time, but in a different time ... Her head was beginning to ache with the effort to make sense out of it all.

She said cautiously, "It may not be here at all, but someone told us there was a grave of two children who died in the fire."

"No, no," said the vicar patiently. "As I explained, the two children were saved, one by the old man and the other by the gardener's boy, or so the story goes."

"Oh," said Lucy, thinking hard. "I'm afraid I didn't

listen very carefully. Is that where the gardener's boy is buried, that little unmarked grave under the tree, where the forget-me-nots grow?"

"Forget-me-nots!" the vicar laughed jovially. "Nettles and nightshade, from what my old sexton tells me. He's always complaining about them."

Lucy frowned nervously. "But he was the one who told us about the forget-me-nots," she said, "and the gardener's boy and the children."

The vicar sighed. "Well, my dear," he said, a little sadly, "he is an old man and perhaps he gets a little confused. He has always insisted to me that it was the grave of two drunken servants who died in the fire. One was the old housekeeper who was overcome by the smoke. They say she had been drinking heavily and had locked herself in her room. The other was her husband who died from a fall; some say that he was mad and that he started the fire. I don't know if there is any truth in it, I'm sure, but the old man insists that the nettles are caused by what he calls 'the evil comin' up from below'. He tells me that weedkiller is useless and he wages a constant battle with them."

Lucy gave up. "It's all beyond me," she murmured. "Here one minute and gone the next; first it's forget-me-nots, then it's stinging-nettles. I wonder if Jamie would understand it."

The vicar considered this remark and decided that it was beyond him too. Children's conversation was so elliptical. He changed the subject.

"And where is your brother today? It's not often I see you alone. And your mother too? I hope the walk did not prove too much for her?"

Lucy's face darkened. "It wasn't the walk," she said, "we are used to walking. It's Jamie; he ... he had an accident, a fall, in the ruins and he's still unconscious. He's been unconscious since Friday night and ... " The words came tumbling headlong and then, before she could stop them, the tears followed. "The doctor says if he doesn't come round soon, they will take him away to the hospital, and I just know he'll never come back!"

She broke off and searched for a handkerchief but in the confusion of setting out, neither she nor her mother had thought of one. She sniffed hard and wondered whether it would be worse to let her nose run or to wipe it on her sleeve.

The vicar bent down and handed her a large handkerchief of remarkable whiteness. "My poor child," he said. "I had no idea! Now do dry your tears and tell me how it happened. There must be something I can do to help."

Lucy took the handkerchief rather gingerly. It seemed almost sacrilegious to use it, like blowing her nose on the white, billowing surplice he wore. But the alternative was worse, so she snuffled gratefully among the snowy folds until she felt more presentable. Then she emerged and said, "He was ... trying ... to save ... them."

As soon as she had said it, she was sorry. It would be so difficult to explain and she was not absolutely sure that there was not some magic in it somewhere. The vicar could hardly approve, even if it was more white than black. But her words had been lost among her hiccuping sobs, and the vicar only said,

"Now, now! you just take things easy, while I go and take this fancy dress off. Then I'll drive you home."

As the little car bowled jerkily along the country road, Lucy and the vicar sat in a companionable silence. There was something she badly wanted to ask him before they reached the house, but she didn't know how to put it. She couldn't think how to ask the question without having to explain it. And yet, she felt that if anyone knew the answer, the vicar might.

At last she coughed nervously once or twice and then said, "Do you think it would be possible to die to save someone who had already died before you were born?"

The vicar took his eyes off the road to glance at her curiously. But the car promptly hit a pothole and he hastily turned his attention back to his driving.

"Well," he began cautiously, "that is what Our Lord did. He died to save all of us, those born before Him and those born after Him. And that is why today is a day of rejoicing for us all."

Lucy sighed, but said nothing. He didn't even begin to understand what she was talking about. But then, why should he? She didn't understand what had happened herself, and she had been there. Jamie was the only one who might know, and he might never come back to explain it all.

What had happened after he went back into the house? The inscription on the monument seemed to prove that Mr Blunden had been there after all. But if so, what had gone wrong? The old man had promised that Jamie would come to no harm, but could she trust him?

The vicar heard her sigh and immediately regretted his tactlessness.

"You must forgive me," he said humbly. "I know it is

not a happy day for you, but we must try to have faith."

"To have faith," thought Lucy; that had been one of the conditions for Jamie, perhaps it was also meant for her. In the beginning, Jamie had said, "You must trust him too," and she had answered, "I will try." Now the time had come. Maybe she couldn't move Highgate Hill, but if Jamie's faith could change the Pattern of the Wheel, then hers would bring him back from the farthest corners of Time.

She closed her eyes and concentrated very hard but it didn't seem to do any good. Perhaps faith isn't like that, she thought. Perhaps it isn't something you force yourself to, a battle that you fight in your mind, but something that comes when you stop fighting, when you admit that you can't manage it alone. And then it just grows in you, like bluebells coming up out of dark decaying despair.

She smiled at the thought, and realized with a start that the vicar had been talking all this time. She tried to look as if she had been listening.

"Somehow," he was saying, "I just cannot believe that anyone could come to harm on such a joyful day as this."

Lucy stared out of the window as they went up the long drive. Everywhere the green buds were breaking, the daffodils trumpeted, and the birds sang. He was right, she thought, it was a day for living, not for dying.

A load of grief seemed to lift from her mind as the Old House came into sight, and as soon as she saw her mother in the doorway, even before she began to wave, Lucy knew that Jamie was all right.

15

LUCY clambered out of the vicar's car before it had quite halted and running across the driveway, she threw herself into her mother's arms.

"Jamie is awake," said Mrs Allen, and the words seemed to spin in Lucy's head. "He just woke up, quite suddenly, about ten minutes ago, almost as if he had just been sleeping. Only I think he was a bit confused because he said, 'I'm sorry, I got held up', as if he had been on a journey instead of falling off a wall."

"Can I go up and see him?" asked Lucy. "Can he talk or will it tire him?"

"I don't think so," her mother sounded puzzled. "He seems to be full of energy and he keeps asking whether he can get up. I hate to keep him in bed when he's fretting so but I've told him he must wait until the doctor has been. I shouldn't like him to have a relapse or something and anyway the doctor will be here in half-an-hour."

Listening to her voice chattering on, Lucy realized with a start that her mother sounded as she used to in the old days, before everything began to go wrong. Their father had always teased her for being talkative, but when the long, sad days came and she rarely spoke at all, Lucy and Jamie had come to long for her rambling sentences.

Lucy stood back a little and looked at her mother wonderingly. Her face was flushed and strangely gay. Lucy hugged her suddenly. "Oh, Mummy," she said, "we do love you!"

Mrs Allen looked down at her and smiled, a rather awkward, crooked smile. "I know," she said, "and I haven't been very fair to you, have I?" She hesitated a moment and then said, "For a while, I thought I had lost Jamie too, and I suddenly realized how much I still have to be grateful for. I shan't forget again, Lucy."

She stooped impulsively and kissed her daughter. "Now run and see Jamie and stop him getting up, while I go and get the vicar away from his car. He's pretending to look at the engine, but I think he's just afraid of intruding."

Lucy went scampering away up the stairs.

Jamie was sitting up and looking very normal. The bed which had been so smooth and white, was now a rumpled mess. There were rejected books all over the place, and the eiderdown was on the floor.

Lucy had pictured a touching, rather tearful reunion after all that had happened, but he only scowled at her as she came in the door and said, "For heaven's sake, why can't I get up?"

"You have to wait until the doctor's been; Mummy said so. But he won't be long," she added hastily seeing that he was about to argue.

Jamie snorted crossly and said nothing.

"Are you ... all right?" asked Lucy cautiously. It seemed a vague enough question to be safe, for she sensed that she was treading upon dangerous ground. If Jamie had forgotten everything, she knew that she would never be able to explain it all, so it seemed wiser not to ask any leading questions.

"Of course I'm all right," Jamie frowned. "Just because I fell off a wall or something ... " He paused, watching Lucy's face, wondering whether she had any idea what had happened to him. It was possible that he had dreamed the whole thing, including Lucy being there. Or if it was real, he could not tell how much she might, or might not, remember. He did not think he could possibly make her understand unless she already knew.

For a few minutes they sat in silence half-watching each other, like boxers looking for an opening. Then Lucy's curiosity won. She took a deep breath and said firmly,

"Well, where have you been, then?"

"Been?" asked Jamie warily.

"You know very well that we should have arrived back at the same time, but you didn't, and you couldn't have been *there*, so where were you?"

Jamie's face split open in a grin of delight. "Then you do remember," he said.

"Of course, *I* remember," said Lucy indignantly. "I didn't go rushing around in burning buildings, falling off walls and getting concussion or whatever. The question is, do *you* remember, and if so, where have you been since sunset on Friday evening? It's nearly two days, you know."

Jamie looked surprised. "Is it really as long as that?" he said wonderingly. "It only seems like a few hours."

But he did not begin to explain. He just sat there with an infuriating far-away look in his eyes.

"Well, don't go broody," said Lucy rather acidly, "tell me!"

"M-m-m ... ?" Jamie seemed to gather his thoughts from a world away as he turned to stare at her. Then he said, "I don't know if I can explain everything ... " and as Lucy began to protest, he went on, "but I'll tell you as much as I remember. Only, you see, it isn't easy to sort it out in my own mind."

He paused, with a frown of concentration, and Lucy tried hard to keep her patience.

"I remember ... " he began, "I remember that I was with Mr Blunden, but I don't know where we were or how we came to be there. I had meant to come straight back as you did ... that was after the stairs gave way and I fell." The awfulness of the memory caught him unawares and he had to struggle to put it out of his mind. "Well, anyway, the old man kept saying that I must go with him and I thought, at first, that I was dead!"

He said it hesitantly as if the memory was embarrassing, and then, as if to justify his own foolishness, he went on quickly, "I had let go of his hand, you see, I couldn't help it or I should have dropped Georgie, and he had said that I should be safe as long as I kept hold of it."

Lucy found it very hard to follow. She wanted to interrupt, to ask a dozen questions, but she sensed that if once she broke the fine black thread of his thoughts, he might never find the broken end again in the darkness of his memory.

"So you see, when I let go, I thought perhaps I would die. But it couldn't be helped, it was just the way it happened ... And when I found I was alone with Mr Blunden in a dark empty sort of place, I didn't like to ask him whether I was dead ... in case he said 'Yes'. So I just said 'I ought to go back to Lucy' because I knew you would be worried if you found you were alone. But the old man didn't seem to hear me. He just said, 'It will not take very long, but I'm certain it will help my case if they see you.'

"Well, I had no idea what he was talking about," Jamie sighed, "but I went with him because I didn't know how to get back here by myself and I thought anywhere was better than being *nowhere*, which was where we seemed to be then.

"The next thing I knew was that we were in a vast room and there was a long, long, table, so long that I couldn't even see the far end of it. It was weird, Lucy, a sort of Alice-in-Wonderlandish feeling because along both sides of the table there were hundreds of lawyers, all in wigs and gowns, and they were all looking at Mr Blunden." Jamie laughed suddenly as he remembered the scene.

Lucy stared at him anxiously. It was hardly what she had expected. She wondered if it could be the after-effects of the concussion. If he gets too excited, she thought, I shall have to call Mummy.

But he stopped laughing after a moment and went on, "Then one of the lawyers stood up, and he began to speak as if he were in court. It was all in legal language and I didn't understand half of it, but I did gather that Mr Blunden had been accused of negligence, something about the line of inheritance being destroyed. He had been struck off, just as he told us, although seeing that he was dead anyway, I couldn't see why it mattered. I mean a lawyer couldn't practise law in Heaven, could he?"

Lucy considered. "Oh, I don't know," she said. "They might let him if it was what he liked doing most. He couldn't sing hymns all the time; he might even be tone-deaf like you."

Jamie thought this dig was beneath his notice. "Well, who would they practise on?" he demanded.

"Each other," said Lucy promptly.

Remembering the long table of lawyers, Jamie thought she was probably right, so he gave up the argument.

"Well, anyway," he said, "the fellow who was doing all the talking was asking them to put the old man's name back on the list again, because he had made amends and put every-thing right. They all started talking it over and I just stood there in a sort of 'cloud of unknowing' because I couldn't see what it had to do with me.

"I was just asking the old man for the umpteenth time whether I could come back, and trying to explain that you would be having kittens, when a voice asked, 'Is this the boy?' and I saw that they were all looking at me. I was afraid they were going to ask me to give evidence, and that I should have to tell them all about the fire ... but all they did was to ask my name. When I told them, they all nodded, and the lawyer said, 'I submit these documents in evidence.' He handed them some papers and they all looked at them and tut-tutted and passed them from one to the other all the way down the table. It was such a long table, I couldn't even see who was sitting at the far end and I thought it would take years for all of them to read everything. But before long, a voice came from the other end of the table; it was loud and clear and I suppose it was the judge. And it said, 'Frederick

Percival Blunden, we have considered the evidence before us and we are satisfied that you have restored the Pattern as it was intended to be.' It went on to say that Mr Blunden would be reinstated as a lawyer, and when he heard that, the old man's face lit up like a Christmas tree. He grabbed my hand and started babbling about courage and fortitude and eternal gratitude. He said a lot of other things too, but I wasn't really listening. He was getting so emotional, I was afraid he was going to kiss me at any moment, and I was racking my brains to think how I could get away.

"Then I realized that we were alone somewhere and the table and the other lawyers had all disappeared. The old man seemed to have calmed down a bit, so I tried to concentrate on what he was saying. But his words were like a loudspeaker van going past in the street; I could hear him, but I couldn't make out what he was saying.

"Everything began to grow misty and confused, my head was spinning, and the next thing I knew, I was sitting up in bed and Mother came and cried all over me and wouldn't let me get up." He paused and shrugged his shoulders. "And if you can make head or tail of all that," he told Lucy, "perhaps you'd explain it to me!"

Lucy thought about it. "It's a pity you didn't listen more carefully to what Mr Blunden was saying."

Jamie frowned. He could not help agreeing with her but he hated to admit it. "You know how I hate being kissed," he said defensively.

Lucy sniffed. "I don't suppose he was going to; I mean, you're not exactly irresistible."

Jamie's frown became a scowl, and Lucy realized with a sudden pang that they were on the point of quarrelling. And half-an-hour ago, she thought, I was afraid I might never be able to talk to him again. She felt a strong urge to kiss him herself, but he looked very hostile and it was more than she dared. She changed the subject.

"I went to the churchyard," she said. "The children's grave has gone," and she told him about the gaudy pink monument.

Jamie was delighted though he did not seem surprised. "Of course, I knew we had changed the pattern," he said, "but it's nice to have proof that things are different."

"No one else seems to have noticed the change," Lucy told him.

"Well, I suppose they wouldn't. After all, if we went back a hundred years to change things, then they must have been changed for as long as anyone can remember."

Lucy found it very confusing. "I don't think I really understand this Wheel of Time business even now," she said.

"Oh, I don't understand it," said Jamie cheerfully, "but then I don't understand television either. But when you've seen it working, you can't help believing in it."

Lucy had to admit that he was right.

"And what about Mr Blunden and the lawyers?" she asked, feeling rather put out that she had not shared this part of the adventure. "I suppose that was just a dream, because of the concussion or something."

Jamie considered. "It was very like a dream," he admitted. "It wasn't real, like Sara and Georgie or even Bella and the

Wickenses. And it didn't seem like a real place, nothing to see or touch. But I think it was real to old Blunden and the others. I mean, it wasn't as if I had dreamed it up inside my head, more as if I had stumbled upon a place where I had no right to be." He struggled for a minute to find a better way to explain it and then gave up.

"Do you think Mr Blunden was ... well ... dead?" asked Lucy awkwardly. "The vicar said the strain was too much for him, that he died soon after the fire."

Jamie's face darkened as he remembered how the old man had suffered. "I suppose he was," he said, "but I'd rather not talk about it."

"The vicar said the Wickenses died too," Lucy told him.

Jamie didn't answer. It was all very well if you thought of them as bad characters in a story, but he could only remember a hysterical old woman screaming "Ghosts!" and a crumpled body at the foot of the stairs. But if they hadn't died, he told himself, it would have been Sara and Georgie and Tom. He made himself think of something else.

"What about Bella and Bertie?" he asked. "Did the vicar say what happened to them?"

Lucy shook her head. "He didn't mention them," she said, "and I didn't like to ask in case he wondered how I came to know about them."

"I rather liked Bella," said Jamie, "she was very pretty."

Lucy snorted. "She was too fat," she said, "and her hair was all mousy ringlets." She thought Sara much prettier with her dark hair and grey eyes.

"She was a bit plump," Jamie admitted, "but I wouldn't

have called her hair 'mousy', more a sort of golden colour."

"She probably married that pop-eyed Bertie," said Lucy. "She would have been an orphan after the fire, so it wouldn't matter if he didn't inherit the money or the house or anything." She pictured them living in a tiny flat, with Bella doing her own scrubbing in a threadbare dress like Sara's, and for a moment she was glad. Then she remembered what it was like to be poor, and it seemed mean to wish it on anyone. So to unwish it she said aloud and rather primly, "I'm sure I hope they were very happy. Maybe Bella went back on the stage or something."

But Jamie was not listening anyway. When she mentioned the house, Lucy had broken his dream and fragments of it came back to him. He sat up abruptly.

"Lucy," he said, "I've just remembered something Mr Blunden said, in between telling me how wonderful I was. It was about the house. He said, 'The house will be safe; the family will go on,' or something like that. And then he said, 'That young fellow, what's-his-name ... ?' "

"Smith," said Lucy automatically.

Jamie ignored the interruption. " '... That young fellow, what's-his-name, will be down to explain everything.' Well, that must mean that they've traced the real owners, or at least that they soon will."

Lucy looked dismayed. "Oh, I hope not!" she said.

Jamie was surprised. "But why?" he said. "It's a shame to see it empty and the gardens all neglected and the pool choked with weeds. It would be super to be able to take the dust sheets off and get the fountain working."

"It would be nice for the house and the new owners,"

Lucy agreed, "but what about us? They wouldn't need a caretaker any more, and we should have to go back to Camden Town." She wondered if it was a judgment on her for wishing Bella and Bertie into poverty. Perhaps *their* descendants would come and turn them all out of the Old House. "I'd rather it fell in ruins," she said miserably, "and the garden was a wilderness, than that we should have to leave it!"

Jamie's face fell. "I hadn't thought of it like that," he said and it was true. He felt that he had known the Old House for a hundred years, which in a way he had, and it had grown to be a part of him. It had never occurred to him that when the Latimers returned, he would have to leave it for ever. "I suppose that if I hadn't helped the old man to put things right," he said slowly, "then they would never have found the rightful owners and we could have been caretakers for ever." He sounded quite indignant, as if he had been grossly deceived.

Lucy thought it would be bad for him to get too worked up, so she said soothingly, "Well, we had to help, anyway, because of Sara and Georgie. At least they lived to grow up and have ordinary lives instead of dying as children. That's more important than us going back to Camden Town."

"I suppose so," said Jamie, "but it does seem a bit hard. After all, we are here and now, and they were a long time ago."

"It depends what you mean by 'time'," said Lucy.

"Oh, don't let's start that all over again!" Jamie sighed and gave the whole thing up. "The only time I want to hear about now", he said firmly, "is lunch-time. So go and tell Mother that I'm starving."

But Lucy had a better idea. Forgetting all about Sara and Georgie, Bertie and Bella, she ran off downstairs, two at a time, to fetch the Easter eggs.

16

EASTER had passed, Low Sunday had come and gone, week followed week until Whitsun was upon them, and still there had been no news.

Lucy and James felt that every day brought Camden Town a little closer, and every day they loved the Old House more. And yet they were not unhappy for their mother was her old self again. When she laughed, or when the sound of her music reached them about the house, they felt that even Camden Town might be a cheerful place. But the spring days were fine and each morning the gardens seemed more beautiful as new flowers struggled up to the sun. Lucy, who had never really had a garden before, worked for hours at a time to clear the choked flower beds and her heart ached when she thought of leaving it all.

And now, at last, the lawyer had come as they had known he would, with a look of triumph on his face and a brief-case full of important documents.

Lucy had taken refuge in the attics. High up under the roof, higher even than the servants' rooms, hot and airless under the roof-tiles, were the store-rooms, silted up with the discarded jumble of several hundred years. Old clothes, old clocks, old toys, old books, which had once been swept along on the strong current of everyday life, now lay in corners like the tide-wrack along the beach, serving only to show where life had been.

All these things had been cherished once for their beauty or their usefulness, or just for the warm familiarity of their presence. Now they were cast aside and forgotten. Just as we shall be, thought Lucy, now that we have served our purpose.

Sometimes, it seemed to her that the house had brought them there for its own ends. We are like the plumbers, she thought, called in because the life-supply has dried up. So we've done all the messy work and now life will start to flow again, there will be people and children and voices, and in the excitement we shall be swept away down the nearest drain to Camden Town. The picture she had conjured up made her smile, but really, she thought, it isn't funny for us.

Down in the caretaker's cottage, the lawyer was talking to their mother. He would be explaining about the new owners, telling her that she would not be needed any longer, generously giving them a month's notice. Why did he have to take so long about it?

She looked around her at the mute, dishevelled toys, the silent clocks. They seemed not so much abandoned as resting, as if with a new generation, a change of fashion, they might find themselves called back into service. Perhaps we could retire to the attics too, she thought hopefully. It is such a big house, they would never miss a small flat up where the servants' bedrooms used to be. We could paste up the old wallpaper and make some new curtains ... But why should the new owners bother with us? We could never explain what we have done for them, and it's not as if we are 'old faithful servants', we have only been here a couple of months. How could we make them understand that in such a little time a house can take hold of your heart as surely as if you had been bound to it for hundreds of years.

"It's all very well for you," she shouted angrily to all the voices which talked unceasingly just out of earshot. "You will belong to someone again, but what about us? Where do we belong?"

The silence that followed was so intense that she knew the voices had stopped, and she felt as if all the ghosts were listening. When they began again, they seemed to be soothing, explaining ... But Lucy was in no mood to be soothed, in no mood to listen to explanations which she could never quite hear. She got to her feet and stamped out angrily, along the passage and down the stairs, ignoring the voices that called from the corners of the rooms.

She reached the first-floor landing where the fainting Bella had lain, charged on down the main stairs, and was on her way to the green baize door when she heard a call that was too strong. Reluctantly she turned and walked back, to the old drawing-room.

It was the blue vase that called her. It stood on its table in a pool of sunlight and Lucy flinched when she thought how close she had come to breaking it. She picked it up carefully and it was warm to touch; she saw how the light shimmered on the myriad cracks in the glaze. She did not know why the sight of the vase should comfort her, but it did. There was something about the endurance of an object so fine and so fragile that seemed to prove something. But as she did not know what it proved, she put it down gently and went off to find Jamie.

Jamie was lying in the long grass by the lake, trying to puzzle out in his mind what it all meant. It was not something he could discuss with Lucy. She would clutch at his vague hopes like a drowning man, and he could not bear her disappointment if he was wrong.

It was foolish to pin so many hopes upon a dream, for it had been a dream, that strange encounter with the lawyers. It had not been real and tangible like the meeting with Sara and Georgie. True, it had been clear and vivid in his mind ... But then dreams often are, he thought, like that time when I dreamed I quarrelled with Lucy and, although I knew it was a dream, I was angry with her all day for the rude things I dreamed she had said.

And yet he could not forget that the voice had said, "Is this the boy?" Which boy? he wondered; surely any boy would have done? But if so, why had they asked his name? And why did Mr Blunden have to find me, why bring us here all the way from Camden Town unless ... But there were footsteps and Lucy was coming along the path. He sat up hastily and began to talk about nothing in particular as if she might have overheard his thoughts.

"Where have you been hiding?" he said. "It's getting quite hot, isn't it? Has he finished yet?"

"In the attic. Yes, isn't it. No, I don't think so," answered Lucy.

She sat down on the grass beside him, and for a while they were both silent. Then she said, "You know that blue vase?"

"The one that's cracked all over?" asked Jamie.

Lucy frowned. "It's not exactly 'cracked'."

"You know what I mean."

"Well, anyway, I nearly smashed it … when you were trying to get the keys from Mrs Wickens … only I couldn't do it."

Jamie said nothing.

"It's strange to think of it being here all this time. It was probably here before Sara and Georgie … " She paused.

Jamie waited to see where she was leading.

"It will probably be here long after we have gone."

"Probably," said Jamie.

Suddenly, the endurance of the vase no longer seemed comforting, and Lucy heaved a sigh. "It doesn't seem fair," she said gloomily.

"Here comes Mother," said Jamie, getting to his feet. He was relieved. He didn't feel up to a discussion about whether life was fair or not. He rather suspected that it wasn't.

Mrs Allen came walking along the path with a thin, anxious-looking man.

"It's not Mr Claverton," Lucy sounded hopeful. "Are you sure he's from the solicitors?"

"It's Smith, the one they keep forgetting. That's probably why he looks so nervous."

He's like us, he doesn't feel he belongs, thought Lucy sympathetically, and resolved to be especially nice to him. She gave him her most dazzling smile and he brightened perceptibly.

"Mr Smith, these are my two older children, Lucy and James." Mrs Allen was carrying the baby who spoiled the dignity of the introduction by blowing bubbles at his brother and sister.

"Mr Smith has brought us some very interesting news about the house," she went on. She looked very calm and Jamie tried in vain to read some hint of their fate in her steady eyes. She sat down on an old garden seat near by, and the lawyer settled himself beside her. Lucy and Jamie sat on the grass and tried to look as if they did not care too much about the news he was bringing.

"I hope you don't mind repeating to the children all that you have told me." Mrs Allen smiled. "I'm sure I should never remember half the details."

"I shall be delighted," and indeed, Mr Smith did seem to relish finding himself the centre of attention. Even the baby was trying to wriggle across to investigate his briefcase.

When the lawyer had finished shuffling his papers, he coughed importantly. "Well now," he said, "to begin at the beginning."

Jamie wished he would begin at the end and save a lot of suspense.

"My firm has for some time been engaged in tracing the records of the Latimer family who have owned this house for many hundreds of years. We had no difficulty with the late owner's father, Matthew, or his grandfather, George Latimer, for in each case the property passed from the father to his only child. However, with the death of Mr Michael Latimer, our late client, who was childless, this branch of the family came to an end.

"Now we found evidence that George Latimer, our late client's grandfather, had a sister, but we could find no record of her after her marriage in the year 1880. It seemed to us most likely that she had died in that year but our searches produced no death certificate. It therefore became necessary to account for her before we could go back any further in our search for heirs. For many months we searched but it seemed that Sara Latimer, or Sara Fletcher as she was then, had vanished without trace."

Jamie, who was politely stifling a yawn, nearly choked on it.

Lucy's eyes grew as round as a fish's. "Sara and Georgie!" she began but she stopped short when she saw that Mr Smith was staring at her.

"Their names are familiar to you?" he asked, his voice incredulous.

Jamie thought fast. "It was the vicar," he said. "He told Lucy about two children who were saved from a fire. Their names were Sara and Georgie."

"There's a big, pink memorial in the churchyard," added Lucy eagerly, "to Mr Blunden, I mean his great-grand-father, because he rescued them."

"Indeed," the lawyer looked very despondent. "I had not heard the story. But then, no one tells me anything. Of course, I have only been with the firm for fifteen years ... " He seemed to sink into gloom.

Oh Lord, thought Jamie, wishing that Lucy had never started this diversion, now he will never get to the point. "Do tell us what you have discovered," he said heartily, "I'm sure it's much more interesting."

Mr Smith brightened. "Ah, yes," he said. "You may well think that it is! You see, we might never have come any closer to the truth but for a letter which arrived mysteriously in our office. It was from Sara herself," he paused, relishing the blank disbelief on the children's faces, before adding, "but it was not, of course, addressed to us personally. The envelope enclosing it bore our address in a fine copperplate hand, but it had no stamp or post-mark, though we found it among our usual morning post. There was no covering note of explanation, no hint of who had sent it, only the old letter which I have here.

"It would seem that George Latimer quarrelled with his sister when she decided to marry a young man who had for many years been a gardener on the estate. Such a marriage would have caused a great scandal in those days when a wide gulf existed between the landed gentry and the working classes, and it seems probable from the difficulty which we had in tracing Miss Sara, that the breach between her and her brother was never healed."

Jamie and Lucy stared at one another and it was all they could do to keep their suppressed excitement from bursting into delight. It seemed so right that Sara should have married Tom, and if Georgie didn't approve, well, he had always been a little snob. Since she had had to choose between them, it was good to know that she had chosen the faithful Tom.

Lucy thought it was the most romantic story she had ever heard. She remembered Tom's words when she had tried to stop him from climbing to the rescue: "Happen I shall be killed, but there's some a person would gladly die for." She wondered if anyone would ever feel like that about her.

But Mr Smith had unfolded the letter. "We will let her speak for herself," he was saying, and with a discreet clearing of his throat, he began to read:

"My Dearest Brother,

In spite of all that has passed, I cannot bring myself to leave these shores without writing to beg you once again that we may be reconciled. Though it is hard, I know, for you to accept my marriage to Tom, yet I think you will be glad to know that we are happy, and that he is all that I would wish my husband to be. You will, perhaps, consider that to be impossible, since to you he is, and will always be, a servant, but I would remind you that he was so by accident of birth and not from any want of virtue or intelligence in himself. We sail in the morning for America, and there I hope he may make for both of us a life in which natural talent may count for more than inherited wealth.

"I need not remind you that I owe my life to his courage, yet it is not from any sense of obligation that I shall devote my future to his happiness. It is because of the great love that has grown between us since we were children together, that I shall go gladly into a new land where he may be allowed to prove his true worth.

"Nevertheless, I would not have you think that in leaving you, I have ceased to love you. For so many years we had only each other, and your place in my heart can never belong to anyone else. It is a great grief to me to be estranged from you, and though you vowed upon my marriage never to acknowledge me again, yet the words were spoken in anger, and I cannot but hope that, as time passes, you will learn to forgive me.

"Whether or not you reply to this letter, I shall continue to write to you and to tell you of the trials and joys that may lie ahead for us. Let me hear from you too, my dearest Georgie, so that I may be assured of your continuing health and happiness.

"More I cannot write, for the mail must go ashore within the hour. Pray for us, as I shall pray for you, and believe me, in spite of all that has passed,

Your ever loving sister,
SARA LATIMER FLETCHER"

As Lucy listened, the lawyer's dry tones seemed to fade and she heard Sara's level, gentle voice. She seemed almost to see her, grown up now but still dark and pretty, her wide grey eyes solemn as she sat in her tiny cabin in the gently rocking ship, writing her last appeal to Georgie before she sailed to a new land where, as Tom had once said, "there was a fine future for a young man who could read and write and was not afraid of hard work."

Even Mr Smith seemed moved by the letter, though he had read it many times before. He sighed before laying it aside and then returned with renewed eagerness to his story.

"This ... er ... touching document," he said, "directed our search to the United States of America where, I may say, inquiry agents are accustomed to moving very swiftly in these matters."

His tone suggested that he considered such speed to be

ill-advised, and certainly, thought Jamie, his worst enemies could not have called Mr Smith 'hasty'.

"Within a very short time, we were furnished with names and dates and, er, photostat copies of documents which proved conclusively that Sara and Tom Fletcher had only one child, a daughter Georgina, who was married in due course to a young American named Allen."

He produced the name with the satisfaction of a good conjurer who has performed a long and complicated sleight-of-hand ending in the appearance of a wriggling white rabbit. But it was all lost on Lucy.

"Alan who?" she asked blankly.

But for once Jamie's brain had raced home ahead of her. This time he knew, while Lucy was still groping in the darkness of her own confusion, exactly what Mr Smith had come to tell them. He knew, without a shadow of doubt, what the voice had meant when it asked, "Is this the boy?"

He felt it would be cruel to spoil Mr Smith's story, but it was hard to keep his joy from breaking out on his face.

"Alan who?" tried Lucy again.

Mr Smith beamed. "Not Alan anybody," he said triumphantly, "but Roderick Patterson Allen, who was your father's grandfather!"

Lucy frowned and thought hard for a moment. Then she shook her head. "That couldn't be right," she said firmly. "I mean, that would make Sara our great-great-grand-mother."

Jamie seized hold of her hands and pulled her round to face him. He almost shook her in his excitement. "That's the whole point, Lucy," he said. "She was, don't you see? She was! And Tom was our great-great-grandfather."

Lucy began to say, "But they weren't much older than…"

Her voice died away as Jamie tightened his grip on her wrists. For a long moment they stared at each other while he willed her to understand and to say nothing. Then he smiled, and his joy spread to her face like the glow of a fire.

"Oh, Jamie," she said, "the house and everything … ?"

"The house and everything!" echoed Mr Smith, with a hearty boom of satisfaction. "The entire Latimer estate will pass to your brother as the senior surviving member of the family."

Lucy looked at Jamie, her mind working feverishly to grasp it all. "It was because of what you did," she said, hardly above a whisper.

"I suppose so," said Jamie, "and yet I never dreamed that it concerned us. I mean, not here and now."

Mr Smith was rambling on. "Of course, when we realized that the surviving descendants had for some time been, to use a colloquialism, 'right under our noses', that they were already living, however unsuitably, in the caretaker's cottage on the estate, well, we were baffled by what seemed to us an incredible coincidence. But upon maturer reflection, it became clear to us that Mr Blunden had all along known, or at least suspected, something of this matter. Indeed, we have since come to believe that he may have been responsible for sending us the copy of Sara Latimer's letter."

"Oh, I guessed it would be him," said Lucy.

Mr Smith smiled indulgently. "We have asked him, of

course, but alas, he is an old man. His mind wanders and his memory has quite gone. That was why he retired," he lowered his voice confidentially, "it was becoming very difficult ... "

"Oh, but it wasn't that Mr Blunden," interrupted Lucy, but she stopped abruptly at a glance from Jamie. "I mean," she went on, "that he didn't seem as if his mind was wandering when he came to see us. He was, well, like a different man ... "

Mr Smith nodded. "He has his good days and his bad days," he agreed. "But then, I have not come to gossip about an ex-partner of my firm. No, indeed, I came only to break the good news to you all. The details I will bring you later, but there is no doubt, Mrs Allen, that the house and the estate will pass to your son, with trustees to take care of his interests until he is of age.

"I realize, of course, that you may not wish to be troubled with a house of this size, and one so remotely situated, but we should be able to find a reliable tenant and the rents can be re-invested in some more suitable ... "

"No!" said Jamie. He said it very loudly and clearly and more authoritatively than he had ever said anything in his short life before.

Mr Smith stopped short and stared at him.

"No," repeated Jamie. This time it was quieter, but just as firm. "You said that the house was mine."

"Of course," – the lawyer looked hurt – "but you must be advised by those with more experience of business."

"I'm sure you know more about business," said Jamie, "but I know more about the house. We've all been happy

187

again since we've been here, and I shall never part with it even though we haven't got a penny beside."

Lucy could have hugged him.

"Oh, there will be an adequate income," said Mr Smith, "even after duty has been paid. I'm sure I'm very pleased to find that you have become so attached to the place, though I don't know what your mother will think."

Mrs Allen had been very quiet all this time, sitting with her face half-hidden against the baby's warm neck, watching Lucy and Jamie as they learned the good news.

Now she said gently, "It is Jamie's house and he must do as he thinks best, but I shall be very happy if he decides we are to stay."

Jamie felt his face glowing. He knew that this day marked a great milestone in his life, and not only because of the inheritance. He understood that in leaving the decision to him, his mother was telling him that he must now begin to take his father's place, so that life could flow on again instead of lying stagnant in a backwater of grief.

Mr Smith looked from one to the other with an attempt at a smile. He sensed that more was being said than the words that were spoken and, as an outsider, he found it a little confusing. He decided to change the subject. "I take it then," he said jovially, "that there has been no trouble with the, er ... " he put one hand in front of his mouth and turning to Mrs Allen, hissed in a loud stage-whisper ... "ghosts?"

The children's mother laughed. "No trouble at all," she said, putting her head on one side to escape the baby who was poking his fist in her mouth. "I'm afraid I don't believe in them."

"No, no, Of course not." He beamed at Lucy and Jamie. "No such things as ghosts, eh, children?"

Jamie said, "It depends on your point of view."

The lawyer looked blank.

Lucy said, "We are all ghosts in a way."

He began to look nervous and she grew confused. "I mean, Jamie and I might be ghosts in a hundred years' time, and no one could be afraid of us, could they?"

Mr Smith's jaw dropped. He was already a little afraid of these rather peculiar children. But he pulled himself together and said, "My goodness, no! Well, my dear Mrs Allen, I must really be off now, if I am to be back in London tonight."

He shook hands with them very solemnly and Jamie and Lucy watched him as he walked with their mother across the lawn back towards his car.

"You can't explain to them, can you?" said Jamie.

Lucy shook her head. "Not even to Mummy," she agreed. "They would think we were joking if we said we should love to see our ghosts again." She hesitated a moment and then asked wistfully, "Do you suppose we ever shall?"

Jamie sighed. "I don't think so," he said. "I don't think the need will ever be great enough, but we shall know that they are here."

There was a long silence; then Lucy said, "Do you suppose Sara knew? I mean, that we were her great-great-grandchildren?"

Jamie laughed. Something about the idea was irresistibly funny, but he tried to take it seriously. "I don't think she could have done," he said at last. "After all, if we hadn't managed to save them, then she wouldn't have been our great-great-grandmother, would she?"

They considered the implications of this possibility, but it was beyond them to make sense of it.

"Who cares anyway about what might have been?" said Jamie recklessly. "We did and she was, and now the Old House is ours and the lake and the fountain and the gardens. And I'm going to run round the whole place without stopping, just to see what it feels like."

And before Lucy could answer, he was off through the sunlit gardens, running and jumping with his arms spread wide as if to gather his whole inheritance to him.

Lucy watched him as he went: across the shaggy lawn where Tom had lain while Sara wiped his smoke-blackened face; along the gravel path where Georgie had stood, kicking the stones with his shadowless feet; past the pink rhododendron bush where they had crouched in hiding from the big man; across the old herb garden, trampling the musk and the madwort underfoot; until he vanished out of sight, behind the creeper-covered ruins of the library.

Then she smiled, and turning went quietly indoors on her way back to the attics. There was just a chance, she thought, now she belonged to the house, that she might be able to make out what the voices of the ghosts were saying.